I Hope God is Laughing:
Confessions of an Imperfect Parent

I Hope God is Laughing:
Confessions of an Imperfect Parent

By Loren Elizabeth Christie

ISBN 978-0-557-92115-7

A portion of the proceeds from the sale of this book will be donated to The Life Center of Long Island, a non-profit, pro-life organization that supports mothers facing crisis pregnancies.

Dedication:

For my children

Prologue

"How to make God laugh: Tell him your future plans." -Woody Allen

I was born in a blizzard with, I am told, a wide-eyed look of shock on my face. Knowing myself, I can guess that I was annoyed, having suddenly slid out of my comfort zone and into the 1970s. If I could have spoken, I bet I would have asked:

"Dude, Where Am I?"

My first hypothetical words seem to be weaved into my adult thinking pattern, as I often feel out-of-sync with the rest of the world.

When I was four, my grandmother's living room was my castle. The windows of my fortress were covered in heavy orange tasseled curtains—very luxurious, I thought at the time. I would sit on my throne—a green high-back chair—and speak regally to no one visible. I would line up my stuffed animal friends on grandma's marble-top table, making them suffer through grand speeches about the importance of using the potty every time.

Back then I believed that when I grew up my home would be the picture of order, and I'd prance through motherhood humming like Snow White before she was scammed.

Thirty years later, perfection is no longer the goal, but some things haven't changed. The same marble-top table is now in my living room, handed down from grandma. My daughter is currently poised on the loveseat, her magic wand extended over Mr. Norman Whiskers, our cat.

"To follow me into the land of the fairies, press the X on your remote control," she says.

I smile while secretly watching her from just behind the door. I am a Generation X'er who left my full-time job to raise three children in the suburbs of Long Island, New York. This is the story of my early parenting adventures. There are sweet, quiet moments when I catch myself staring at my children in awe of their preciousness. Other times, I feel completely off-balance. My patience is gone and I'm left biting my own fist in frustration, threatening to call "THE MAN" (whoever that is).

When it comes to juggling roles, experts advise parents to seek balance. Overall, I think that "balance" is a GOOD word. It used to be my friend, but now I can't find it anywhere. I look under the bed; I stick my hand into the creases of the leather couch; I go out to the car and check under the back seats. Maybe it escaped when I opened the door? I contemplate grabbing a bag of Cheetos and walking down the block, calling it by its name. That would be bizarre, and I'll certainly be arrested for neglecting dwarfs, (especially a certain Bigfoot dwarf I live with who likes green permanent markers.)

It's no use. Balance is gone. I'm not sure why it left me. Today, I start spring cleaning in hopes that I might find Balance, or bribe it and convince it to return to my home. In preparation for this cleaning spree, I travel to Home Depot and buy a cart-load of hazardous materials that require latex gloves and disposable rags. Have you read the fine print on heavy-duty cleaners? I open the windows to prevent myself from becoming the first Spring Cleaning Martyr, taken out by the fumes.

First, I tie up the children. Just kidding ... maybe. Okay, first, I occupy the children. Then I snap on my gloves. This makes me feel ... empowered. HAHAHA! (Note to self: Never drink Robitussin without the dosage cup.)

I started a book club recently in an effort to regain Balance in my life. It's a hard core reading club, man. We only read classics that require two extra-strength Tylenol per chapter. After each book is done, we dye our hair green and go moshing, (not really, but a good idea, right?)

"Anna Karenina" was the first book on our list, and I liked that one. Now we're reading "Les Miserables," unabridged, and this novel is literally kicking my arse. Fourteen hundred pages and I have no time or energy to read it, especially with sick, crazed dwarfs running around my home. So, I've been listening to it on my iPod while I clean. I cannot find the actual book anywhere.

"How does this happen?" I ask of the gas station attendant. I stop him from filling my tank because I just realized that my wallet is missing from my bag. He does not know how I came to be such a silly, balloon-headed woman, but he thinks I'm charming enough to let me go home and get it even though I owe him three dollars.

Balance left me, but Charm is still my friend.

Now, I'm back to cleaning. I start with the windows. Then I move on to the stainless steel appliances. I'm feeling better until I open the cupboard. Oh, no. I slam the door shut.

There is a quarter of a bag of Nestle chocolate chips left over from cookies that I was supposed to bake. I thought I purged the house of chocolate in preparation for Lent. It's just me, three dwarfs and chocolate alone for the next 10 consecutive hours. This is a very toxic environment for a Catholic attempting to fast. God knows I'm no match for the coco bean. I hope He is laughing. It doesn't end well. I finish off the bag and black out.

I'll blame this Lenten slipup on my loss of Balance and excess of dwarfs. The good news is my house is cleaner and now officially "chocolate-free." As penance, I promise to finish "Les Miserables."

Darkness eventually comes and a typical morning in a modern mother's life follows. Six-year-old Big Brother, four-year-old Princess and two-year-old Baby Bigfoot see me—and they are hungry. I gulp and start my day. If I am lucky, my husband, whom I lovingly refer to as "The Milk Man" for his efficiency in bringing home dairy products, will have stocked the fridge with the essentials: a dozen eggs, a gallon of milk, orange juice, sandwich bread, peanut butter and jelly. Then, all will be right in my world.

"Ladies and Mommies! Welcome to the big circus!"

Big Brother makes this announcement in his pajamas as I'm entering the den. The room is transformed into a makeshift circus ring, complete with a Spiderman tent and Native American drum, the latter to help introduce amazing acts, of course.

"I am now an acrobat," he continues. "Little sister is Bonzo the clown, and Baby Bigfoot is the bouncing ball!"

The show goes on for several minutes while I fry "eggy bread" in the kitchen for the circus employees, and periodically shout "Wow!" as unbelievable stunts involving my leather sectional continue. I come to the baby gate that separates the den from the kitchen holding two plates of French toast.

"Now, I would like to introduce our special guest," my son says to his sibling audience, who are also enthusiastic circus participants.

"It is MOMMY the great elephant!"

And so my day begins, and my stumble through motherhood continues. My pen is in my sweater pocket, and I know I have paper somewhere … I guess a paper towel will do. I wonder what will become of all my notes on family life. Will great discoveries about motherhood occur as a result of my research? In this journey I've discovered that when I think I am at my wit's end, and have even threatened to call "THE MAN," somehow I still haven't run out of love.

Contents

Chapter 1

My Work Requires Protective Clothing

On any random weekday, as soon as my eyes open in the morning, I'm pulled back into the whirlwind of requests and needs. "Mommy, Breakfast? Mommy, Snack? Mommy, drink? Mommy, lunch? Mommy, snack again? Mommy, have to go potty. Mommy, change my diaper. Mommy, can you get me…? Mommy, you need to … AHHHH!" You get the idea. I figure I better do something before my transformation into an octopus is complete.

I stop the three of them in their duckling-like tracks.

"What mommy needs is to use the restroom, without assistance or conversation companions. Then she must wash her face with real water AND soap, brush her teeth, (not with her finger as she is running out the door), and eat a meal, sitting down."

Blank stares follow my announcement, followed by a very authentic depiction of biblical wailing and gnashing of teeth outside the bathroom door. In the evening I'm on the cell phone recounting the madness of the day, while changing Baby Bigfoot's diaper, a habit that should be outlawed in New York State.

"Then the baby gripped my hair so hard ... I was screaming for him to let go, and he just laughed. It was almost sadistic ... and while I was helping Princess off with her Snow White costume, her hand came up and hit me right in the eye. Yup, the same one I hurt last year. I swear I need a body guard to protect me from my children. Hey, that would make a great Jerry Springer Show topic ..."

My friend is sympathetic, and it feels good to vent. She says she's sending me a little package of some stuff she no longer needs now that her children are older. She won't tell me what's going to be in the box, and I start carrying on like a preschooler trying to crack her silence.

"When you get it, it will make sense," she says. "Trust me."

I hate it when my mommy friends play Yoda. Gradually, the conversation moves somewhere into the realm of frozen corpse celebrities.

"I'd only do that partially," she says.

"What? How partially?" I ask, pulling off the baby's diaper with one hand.

"Like just cryogenically freeze my head and then attach it to a new, younger body," she explains.

I am in mid-laugh when it happens: sniper pee. Guess where it hits me this time? Straight up the shirt and ... that's right!

Next I'm rolling on the floor, gagging next to the discarded cell phone. I pull five wipes out in rapid succession and scrub my tongue. Then I pick the phone back up and end the conversation.

A couple of days later the package arrives in the mail. I rip open the box and frown. It's addressed to the attention of "The Stay-at-Home Mom." I think the sender is trying to annoy me. But then I pull out a football helmet, mouthpiece and poncho. Attached to the top of the helmet is a sticky note with my friend's scribbling.

"This is to wear to work."

They're Laughing at THE MAN!

Outside Princess's dance class, Baby Bigfoot is choking on a cookie.

"Hands up!" I say, and he raises his arms, still coughing, with a confused expression.

My daughter's dance teacher passes us.

"Hands up!" she tells him.

He lifts his arms up again. Five minutes later he's choking on juice.

"Oh, oh, it went down the wrong pipe; that's what happens when you laugh with food in your mouth." I say.

Baby Bigfoot anticipates my next sentence and like Pavlov's dog, he raises his hands above his head giggling through the cough. At least he's prepared for any future arrests.

Why do I tell him to do that? I wonder.

I stop the dance teacher as she passes a second time.

"Why do you say 'hands up' when someone coughs?" I ask her.

She pauses and shrugs. "My mother always said it," she explains.

Isn't it weird that we carry on sayings and traditions, like programmed robots, not even knowing why? This thought occupies my mind while I watch my Princess twirl across the floor in the next room.

"The Man" is another unexplainable legend in my family.

(Flashback to 1977)

My Mom: "Loren, Don't touch! Hey! The Man is watching."

My Reaction: Frozen terror.

I imagined this man. He was big, that's for sure, with a black hood that hid his face and long, knotted fingers reaching out to grab kids.

(Fast-forward to 2010)

Me: "You better stop running around now, here comes The Man."

My kids' reaction: "LOL Mom."

Who is The Man and what happened to his effectiveness?! He started losing authority when my younger brother was about two years old. Then mom had to call backup for The Man.

(Flashback to 1980)

Mom: "Put that down Robbie, you're going to get hurt. Here comes The Man! Oh, oh! Do I have to call the police?"

I corner my extended family at lunch. At the table sits my mother, aunt and grandmother.

"Mom, who is The Man and why do mothers say 'Hands up' when kids choke?"

My mom looks at my aunt, and they both shrug.

"We don't know. We just heard it from grandma." my mother says.

"Where did you get those ideas, grandma?"

My grandmother shrugs.

"I don't know. My mother and grandmother used to say those things."

"I think it's time to retire The Man. After about 100-plus years of lurking around near naughty children, he's lost his edge.

"What is this world coming to?" I ask my family, laughing. Then I raise my arms up in the air. (I'm choking on my ham sandwich.)

"Oh, oh, it went down the wrong pipe. That's what happens when you try to talk with food in your mouth," says grandma.

Congratulations Parents! It's a Sponge

I have Pink Floyd to thank for some of my early language acquisition skills. I remember sitting on the floor, hearing the strange and magical chiming of clocks blasting on my parents' reel-to-reel and saying "clock." My father calls my children "little sponges." He's right; this is a lesson that he learned from raising both me and my brother. It's amazing what children absorb from their environments.

Today my little sponges are dressed as such, in SpongeBob SquarePants bathing suits and matching flip-flops. We're on our way to the "mommy beach," a safe, shallow place on the Long Island shoreline. In between Elmo movies, I like to blast CDs in the mini van. I'm playing a song from the Talking Heads, a classic band from my youth. I look in the rear-view mirror and see bobbing heads in the back seat. The kids are singing in their car seats. Even the baby is jerking his head from side to side. Apparently, they all like the music. I'm so amused that I almost hit a parked car; I can't stop looking at their hysterical expressions. Big Brother is on air guitar; his sister is hitting the imaginary drums on the arms of her car seat.

"I WISH YOU …WOULDN'T SAY THAT … NOW JIMMY'S COMING OVER!" They sing at the top of their lungs.

At the beach Big Brother turns into "safety cop."

"Oh No! Sister's taking a deeper step into the water! Mama! Now she's sitting down in the large waves!"

He's jumping in frantic distress and sand is scattering everywhere.

"Relax," I say. "She's fine."

I'm thinking that he's a little clone of his Dad, who nearly drowned as a child and has grown up to be an "ocean alarmist." I sit on the blanket, wondering if this characteristic is inherited or if he picked it up through observation. Meanwhile, the baby is climbing on me to stay off of the sand. Hating the feeling of sand is definitely inherited; I'm told I cried the first time I stood in it. As the waves inch toward my feet, I conclude that the answer must be people are affected by both genetics and environment … and that woman to my left should really not be wearing a bikini.

Tonight I pass Princess' room and stop to listen. I can't believe what I'm hearing. She's rocking back and forth, hugging her pillow, singing Talking Head's lyrics:

"I can't sleep my bed's on fire! Don't touch me I'm a real live wire! Psycho Pillow, pesticide, Ba ba baba ba ba. Better, run, run, run away!"

I think it's time to start playing some Baby Einstein in the car before the kids turn into mindless SpongeBobs.

St. Therese Dines at Friendly's

I plan a whole day of fun with the kids (to secretly teach them about their Catholic faith). Part one is a trip to a beautiful park called The Shrine of Our Lady of the Island. We complete a Rosary walk and view life-size Stations of the Cross. The kids call this place "The Magic Garden."

In the part of the woods called the Avenue of the Saints, Princess is enthralled by a statue of St. Theresa. I buy her a book about the saint in the gift shop, and she picks out a small statue of her. Then I take them to Friendly's for dinner. Once seated, my daughter pops the plastic saint on the table beside her menu and crayons.

"St. Theresa is very hungry, Mommy. She wants some fries." Princess is dead serious, but her older brother is in stitches. I hush him. Meanwhile, Baby Bigfoot is blowing bubbles through the straw in his milk, spilling it everywhere as he scribbles in purple on my jacket. Then, my daughter tells the waitress and all surrounding strangers about her new plastic friend, St. Theresa.

"St. Theresa loves everybody, and gives flowers to everybody she loves," she says.

"Oh, that's lovely," coos the waitress, winking at me.

This little girl is so totally unique; she fascinates me. I hope she is always strong enough to be herself.

After ice cream sundaes, we're back at home in the bathroom, getting ready for bed. St. Theresa is on the counter watching teeth get brushed. Then the kids change into their pajamas.

"Hahaha! I see your pee-pee maker," Princess shouts in a sing-song voice.

In my sternest tone, I call her by her full name.

Big Brother's underwear is on wrong, and the frequency of this mistake frustrates him.

"My parts are always falling out! STOP LAUGHING!" He yells at his sister.

"AHHHH!" Baby Bigfoot growls at his sister, imitating his brother's anger. He's busy wrapping us all up in an unraveled roll of toilet paper.

"Oh, oh, here comes The Man!" I shout, thoroughly worn out from a day of "fun."

"Put on your pajama pants now and stop it!" I tell him.

"Miss Princess," I say as she is laughing and poking her brother in the back with her toothbrush, "YOU stop teasing!"

"Oh, shock-a-dibbles!" exclaims Princess. This is one of her made-up curses.

"Hey Big Brother," she continues in a muffled voice as I pull her shirt over her head, "Wanna see my cooley?!" She flashes him and laughs. He falls on the bathroom floor in a fit of giggles.

"That's it! The Man is watching you all through that window!" I say, forcing my face into an expression of anger. All three children glance toward the window, then laugh.

"Those parts of you are private, just like your brother's parts are private." I continue. "You don't go around pulling down your pants. The police will arrest you." (Please understand readers, sometimes I need to call in backup for The Man.)

The laughing ceases as the children glance at each other, appearing worried.

"Oh, no!" Big Brother whines. "What about all those times I took a bath with my baby brother and sister?"

"That doesn't count," I say, still frustrated from all the horsing around.

"It's only okay to show your cooley to your family and friends," Princess informs us in an authoritative tone.

Big Brother looks at me for verification. "Mommy, is that true?"

"Yes, …Um, … No! What? I don't know; it's time for bed." I say, truly confused.

Five minutes after they hit their pillows, they are sleeping, looking angelic once again. Their innocence is so refreshing and funny. As I stand in Princess' doorway and stare at her grasping her little plastic statue, asleep with the blanket tucked up under her chin, I think a bed time prayer. I hope my children always remain so unabashed in showing the world their faith, but not their … parts. A strange prayer, but considering the day's odd mix of events, not an inappropriate one.

Playboy for Kindergarteners

Big Brother is hiding a book behind his back as he ascended the steps toward his bedroom. I ask him if he wants me to read it aloud. He says no and won't explain why.

"I just want to look at it, under my covers, alone."

"Okay," I say slowly, reassuring myself, mentally, that my house is free of porn magazines. Big Brother takes his "secret" book into his room, and shuts the door. I hear a click; that means he locked it.

Now the suspense is killing me. What in the world is my kindergartener reading? Trying to give him some "big boy space," I decide to wait until he's sleeping before I peek. He doesn't know that the key to his door is resting on top of the molding.

I return to the den. Milk Man is hoarding the remote, flipping from "Hannity and Colmes" to CNN. On the news, Sarah Palin is boarding a jet, on her way overseas to meet Heads of State, with her newborn in tow.

"Wow," I marvel. "How does she get around like that, care for children, and look so 'put together' at the same time?"

I'm thinking out loud, which is hazardous to one's self-esteem in my house. Milk Man laughs.

"You can't even get to a Citibank with three kids," he responds.

He thinks he's so witty, sitting there, in his boxer shorts, eating a Snicker's bar in front of the television. He's a scene straight from the cover of a romance novel (written in Braille). I'm about to send him out for a gallon of milk so I can confiscate the remote control when I remember Big Brother's mystery book.

We sneak up the stairs. Opening the door gingerly, we peer inside Big Brother's room. He's asleep, clutching the "forbidden" book in his hands. We tip toe in and slide it ever so carefully away from his fingers. Safely out in the hallway, I turn on the light. The secret book is "The Little Mermaid." I'm confused.

"He was acting too embarrassed to show me the book. It was like he was reading "Playboy." I couldn't imagine what he had."

Milk Man laughs.

"This is kind of like "Playboy" for kindergarteners," he says, flipping through the pages.

"WHAT?" I shout, forgetting I might wake kids.

"Well, in the mind of a little boy, Ariel is pretty hot," he explains.

Going back into Big Brother's room, my husband slides the book under his bed, and pats my sleeping son on the head.

"That's my boy!" he whisper-shouts.

We both start laughing because he's a doofus. I order him to put some pants on and go buy a gallon of milk.

"Yes dear," he replies. Sometimes I think I married a kindergartener.

Golden Love

"We ourselves feel that what we are doing is just a drop in the ocean. But if that drop was not in the ocean, I think the ocean would be less because of that missing drop. I do not agree with the big way of doing things." -Mother Theresa

I am feeling suddenly insignificant today, and a little morbidly introspective, which sometimes happens if you're a stay-at-home mom with a touch of PMS. Plucked from my social network and previous sense of identity, I am forced to readjust in a domestic cave. Don't get me wrong, I love my cave, and I couldn't wait to nest in it. I just feel disconnected at times from the rest of the world. Then I read my horoscope online. I think my laptop may be psychic, or maybe it's just bugged. It's exactly what I need to hear from someone, or in this case, something, but still I'm skeptical.

"You are a superstar. Go You," it reads.

"Yeah Right. Go Me!" I say aloud to the screen.

Next I'm doing laundry, surrounded by mounds of white sheets and beige towels. I'm folding and folding. This mundane task always launches me into Plato-esque contemplation; I think it may be a result of the bleach fumes. I wonder if I'll be doing laundry during my last second on Earth, and if it will really matter if Milk Man has his teddy bear dress socks clean when I croak. Sifting out the superhero underwear for Big Brother, I start to think about my contribution to society as a whole. Will I be forgotten like the white sock under the dryer? How big of a ripple do I really make on the ocean we call life?

These ideas are as deep as the mountains of clothes that I carry upstairs. I pause to eavesdrop on Princess and Baby Bigfoot. She's in his room, wearing her Snow White dress and sprawled out on his toddler bed.

"Okay, baby brother. Now, I'm Snow White and you are the handsome prince, Carlos. I have fallen asleep because the angry witch put a spell on a shiny red apple from Waldbaum's."

She puckers her lips and motions to the baby to come closer to her.

"You have to get over here and kiss me. No, baby brother, not that way, silly! Over here!"

The baby wobbles toward her. Leaning over and almost losing his balance, he gives her an open-mouthed, slimy kiss.

"Mmmwah," he exclaims, smacking his mouth on her cheek. Princess giggles.

"Thank you prince Carlos! Oh, my! I have waked up! You broke my evil spell with your golden love, just like Mommy."

Princess looks up and sees me in the hallway. I ask her what golden love is. She shrugs.

"It's just special mommy love. You take me to dance class, and you put it in my food when you say, 'Please *eat this, I made it with love.*'" She changes her voice to do a high-pitched mommy impersonation.

I walk away from the room feeling very important. Giants may have golden eggs, but I have golden love. Go Me!

Generation Text

Big Brother has to be at the bus stop in 20 minutes and he's playing a computer game, shoeless, and has bed-head. To complicate matters further, he didn't bother to wear underpants and his shirt is on backwards. I move him to the table for breakfast; he protests.

"Oh! I just got this baby hot-waxed, Mom!"

I stop, hearing only the "hot-waxed" part.

"What does that mean?" I ask. I'm not a morning person. Still groggy, I think my little boy is unknowingly being vulgar. He repeats himself, then explains.

"The computer, Mom! Baby Bigfoot shut off the power and I had to reboot the whole thing."

I'm staring at this little alien of mine, who seems to have been born comfortable with computers. I have a master's degree in educational technology. What does that mean? I'm not afraid to send an attachment in an email, and I don't have to read the instruction booklet for my digital video camera. Really, this course of study just eliminated my fear of computers.

My kids, on the other hand, were born with computer mouses in their hands. Princess navigates Barbie's website like a pro, taking the virtual rock star that she created to an imaginary American Idol competition, where she sings "*Oops! I Did It Again,*" for a simulated screaming audience. Big Brother is studying marine biology on National Geographic Kids. Baby Bigfoot thinks he's conducting very important toddler business, putting his little chubby pointer finger on the mouse pad of my laptop, and actually getting the arrow to move on the screen. The first time I saw a computer mouse was in college, and it took me two weeks to control it. Times have changed, and last time I checked, I wasn't that old. Technology seems to be advancing quickly.

Cell phones are another invention that baffles me. Baby Bigfoot walks around the house with toy versions on both ears at once. Who knows what phones will look like when my kids become teens. They'll probably be able to stop speaking altogether and just text all of the time. As an old lady I'll be saying things like:

"I remember the good old days, when people had verbal conversations."

Don't get me wrong, I think cell phones are convenient, but what a distraction! Personally, I hate being tracked.

"Go out for a few hours by yourself," Milk Man will say on evenings when I need Calgon to take me away. So I do, and exactly one hour later my cell phone rings. It's him asking me where I am, what I'm doing, and when I'm coming home. That's why I let the battery run out all of the time.

Tonight, the whole family is at the dinner table. I tell my children a tale about the hardships of my childhood, back in the 1980s.

"Wow! You lived in the 1900s!" Big Brother exclaims, awed.

"Yes," I say, clearing my throat with importance as I begin my wise story. "When I was your age, I had to use the pay phone to call home if I needed my parents."

Princess looks shocked.

"What's a pay phone?" she asks Big Brother in a whisper.

He leans toward her ear and explains in a hushed tone.

"That is a phone with an ATM machine inside of it. When you typed in the phone number, there was a choice on the screen of English or Spanish. Then, you had to put money in the slot to talk."

Big Brother turns to me, smiling. He knows everything.

I continue. "When I met daddy, beepers were popular. His friends tried to show me how to use one the day we met."

Again, my daughter's brow crinkles in pensive confusion. She looks at Big Brother, who explains this one aloud.

"Mommy was in the street and daddy was in a car with his friends. Daddy was going to hit her so he beeped the horn and he missed. Right, Dad?"

Milk Man has a vindictive smile on his face. He's loving this set up right now.

"Yes, son. I swerved the car, and when I woke up from the coma, I was married."

"What's a 'coma'?" Big brother asks.

Princess puts her hand up, using her most commanding tone. "I know, I know. A coma is mommy's golden love spell."

Parenthood Requires the Naked Truth

"Craft must have clothes, but the truth loves to go naked."
-Thomas Fuller

The idiom "the naked truth" supposedly refers to a fable from the 16th century in which Truth and Falsehood go bathing. Falsehood then dresses in Truth's clothes, and Truth, refusing to take another's clothes, leaves naked. My children often catch me off guard, usually with questions that seem a little beyond their years. Occasionally, they also challenge me when I'm half-dressed. Therefore, in the Christie house, the idiom means being honest while naked, literally at times.

A case in point is when I'm in the middle of getting dressed and Princess enters the room, unannounced. Luckily, on this particular day, I have a chance to put on underwear before the interruption. Curious, she strolls past me, singing the chorus of the opening song in Disney's "Beauty and the Beast." Meanwhile, I'm trying to match my clothes. Looking at me from the corner of her eye, she pauses her song and presses my chest with her pointer finger asking,

"Mommy, what are these?"

I move past her into my hanging clothes for privacy and to slip on my shirt. They're called breasts," I answer from the closet as I shut the door. I hear a muffled "Oh." Then, moments later, she knocks.

"Yes, Can I help you?" I sound a little annoyed, rushing to put on my shoes on the closet floor. Alone time is a commodity in the Christie household.

"Mommy, um, Mom, do I have breastus too?"

"Yes," I respond from behind the door, laughing.

"Oh," she replies. Through the crack in the door I see her lifting up her sweater to investigate.

A few moments pass, and I wonder what her little mind is thinking as I pull my shirt over my head.

"Mommy, um, Mom, what do breastus do?"

I open the closet door, fully dressed. I feign confusion, getting her to repeat "breastus" again just for kicks, and to buy myself some time to correctly word my response. Bending down to her level, I tell the princess that breasts are for feeding babies and they also make a lady look pretty. She is quiet for a moment.

Her lips form that little side smirk and Princess exclaims, "Oh Mommy, that's re-dick -oo-lus!" You do not feed Baby Bigfoot your breastus! That's so silly! He drinks bottles."

"True, but some ladies do something called breastfeeding. Mommy does not." Then comes the inevitable: "Why?"

I explain that I didn't want to breastfeed, but every lady has that choice when she has a baby. Princess is following me all around the bedroom during this conversation, dragging her flip flops on the floor. Now she begins a dialogue with herself, or perhaps, an imaginary lady, and falls into her own little world of make believe.

It's my turn to invade her privacy, as she flip-flops down the hall to her own room and shuts the door. I put my ear against it, curious. I hear:

"Oh, hello, Barbie of Fairytopia. Yes, we're both ladies. We're not boys. When I'm a grown up lady I will not feed my breastus to babies, that's DISGUSTING! I will just use them to look beautiful in my lovely dresses."

What Transforms Us

*"There are two ways to live: you can live as if nothing is a miracle;
you can live as if everything is a miracle." - Albert Einstein*

I go into Princess' room to tuck her into bed. Her tea table is set for several guests, (some sit on the table). I end up spending ten minutes eating plastic muffins with a duck, an elephant, a mermaid, a fairy, Biddy Baby, and St. Therese of Lisieux.

"Everyone is invited to my party, Mama, because I love everybody," Princess announces serving me invisible tea. Imagine having her point of view, I think. What could I do, or become if I were that open-minded as an adult? I've been trying to explore and deepen my prayer habits. Tonight, I notice how my daughter prays, (at four years old).

"Let's say a bed time prayer." I suggest.

"Okay, Mama. I have this card that I want you to read." She pulls a prayer card out from under her pillow. St. Therese of Lisieux is pictured on the front.

So I read the prayer while she quietly recites it line by line in her sweet little voice. I have this feeling at that moment, watching her press her tiny hands together and look up at the ceiling, that the room is surely filled with angels.

"St. Therese, the Little Flower, please pick me a rose from the heavenly garden and send it to me with a message of love; ask God to grant me the favor I thee implore and tell Him I will love Him each day more and more. Amen."

"What special favor do you want St. Therese to pray for?" I ask in a hushed voice.

"Um, to help me clean up my messy room." She whispers back.

"Oh, wow. That's a good one." I say, smiling.

Walking down the stairs I'm still thinking about how wonderful her innocence is, how pure her heart is. I want to be just like her when I grow up.

As a Catholic, I often struggle in my faith journey. In an effort to increase my prayer habits and strengthen my faith, I start a secret habit. It's inspired by my great grandmother, Santa LaCapria. I always admired was her peaceful countenance. I would look at her and think: I want to get that serene. I want to show that type of demeanor to my children. How did she maintain that countenance?

Looking back, I think that it has everything to do with her prayer habits. She often prayed in my presence, but she never forced me to join her. Every night at five o'clock, she'd pray the Rosary, pacing in front of the television. She prayed for everyone on the news.

To emulate her I start praying for people in my thoughts everywhere I go. For example, when I'm driving, I try to wish every car, every person on the street, blessings. What I discover after doing this for a while is that prayer can be exhausting, distracting, and slightly dangerous while driving. It distracts me from patterns of negative self-talk, from focusing on worries and personal problems. It takes me outside myself, and helps me put my own life into perspective.

Princess is calling me back up to her room. She wants me to turn on her Tinkerbell movie. I press play, and she snuggles down into her covers with a broad smile. Tinker bell is shooting pixie dust.

"That's special prayers for all the fairies, Mama," my daughter says, referring to the sparkling dust.

Meanwhile, downstairs, my husband is walking in the door from a long day at work. He hands me a bouquet of mini-roses. I'm surprised, thinking of the prayer Princess insisted we say at bed time.

"What's this for?" I ask?

"They were selling them at work after the school play, and I thought of you." He explains.

This is how prayer comes full circle.

Chapter 2

I Went To College To Be an Elf

"The mouse that hath but one hole is quickly taken." - Herbert

Who would have guessed that motherhood is a heavy test of one's critical thinking skills? The first two weeks after resigning from my full-time job, I feel like I'm playing hooky. As time goes on, however, I realize the ways in which my education enriches me in this multi-faceted role.

Motherhood requires a certain amount of forethought in every situation. If you make a promise, you better follow through, because little minds do not forget. If you chose to say "no," better brace yourself both mentally and physically. If a parent doesn't set guidelines and limits, he or she will become a tortured slave. I'm not kidding, just watch one episode of *Super Nanny*. A parent needs to be in control, *and* give children room to grow. There are no lunch breaks unless naps are taking place; this job is a 24-hour shift. There is a good amount of irony in the fact that staying home to raise children is no romp in the playground; you think it's going to be like a vacation until you try it. A full-time parent must be a detective, a maid, a cook, an architect, a teacher, a nurse, a policeman, and on a really tough day, maybe even a fireman. (No joke, I have a gas stove.)

Today I spend three hours putting together a train table for the boys. One hour is spent with the drill in reverse, because I assemble it backwards. Meanwhile, Big Brother is at school, Baby Bigfoot is safe in his pack n' play and Princess is sitting in the empty box, mimicking my mumbled curses.

"You're a good driller!" she says, boosting my self-confidence. Finally, the table is finished. I flip it over and attach the top.

"How did you learn how to do that Mommy? Did the teacher have you make a train table in science class when you went to college with Steve from Blue's Clues?"

I look over at her, out of breath from moving the huge toy. "That's exactly right! I went to college to learn how to put together toys … like a big … elf." I say, sarcastically, underestimating her sponge-like tendency to absorb things I say and do.

Princess smiles. "A-xact-ily Mommy!" Then, after a pause, she asks, "Did the teacher give you stickers for being good at the job of Mommy?"

"Um, no. I wasn't a mommy then, I was a girl. Besides, college doesn't give out stickers, they just take your money."

Princess looks surprised, but soon forgets the conversation because there are plastic bubbles to pop. After dinner, the phone rings while I'm giving the baby a bath. Princess answers it like she's not supposed to do. I'm leaning over the tub when I hear:

"No, *LOREN* is not here ... that's so ri-dick-oo-lus! That WAS my mommy's name when she was a girl, like me, and played Barbies. Now she is called Mommy or Mom ... She works as a big elf in our house, and she has no dollars in her wallet because college took all her money. *You* should have given her stickers because 'Mommy' is a very A-portant job. Good-even-ing."

Click.

I call her into the bathroom by her full name and she marches in, reluctantly, staring at the floor.

"Who was that on the phone that you are NOT supposed to pick up ever?!" I say, sternly.

"Um, that was Lie-U Post college. They asked if Loren is here and if she can give dollars."

I cannot believe this child is only three years old. I can't stop laughing. *Delegation*, another skill of a stay-at-home mom, comes in handy at this moment. "Okay," I say, "from now on you are the official household receptionist. Congratulations on your excellent telemarketer handling skills."

"YAY!" she shouts, running off in her purple Tinker bell slippers. Then, a few seconds later, Princess calls out to me from the den:

"Mommy, What's a household skeptionist?"

Taking Children To Church Makes You Sin

When was the last time I actually heard, and retained, one thing that was said at Sunday Mass when my children were with me? I can't really remember, but I think it was sometime during 2003, when my oldest was still a newborn. Confined to his removable car seat, he was still too small to create holy terror and make church very stressful for me and my husband. Now that five years have passed, one would think that it is safe to go peacefully, but like good Catholics, we've created two more terrorists over that time. We're looking at another five years of sinning until the youngest learns something that resembles civility.

Yes, church makes me sin. The kids pull, punch and nudge each other, fighting over a secret stash of pretzels until the bag rips and the contents scatters like shrapnel in the pews, hitting old ladies and their snoozing spouses. They speak at inappropriate times, shouting lamentations about going home. They drop the kneeling cushion on my toes.

Is it too much to ask of three children to sit quietly for one hour? The kids to the right are doing it. Why aren't mine? What's that mother's secret? I wonder incessantly instead of paying attention. Filled with thoughts of parental jealousy, I miss the homily. Even though there's only about 15 minutes to go, they become an eternity. My husband and I are in a non-verbal battle over whether or not the kids should be taken out of the building, right now! It starts with glares, then nudges, until attempts to leave are silently blocked by the spouse who is less stressed-out. This non-verbal struggle sometimes leads to arguments later about discipline judgment.

Some stodgy guy to my left, meanwhile, is glaring at my children who are pretending the missalettes are their Easter bonnets. I shoot eye-daggers back. Children belong in church, too. I feel angry at those who make them, and me, feel unwelcome. I'm sitting beside a statue of the Blessed Mother, ready to take on this elderly man in polyester pants; I think something is wrong with this picture.

Maybe the pastor will invest in one of those sound-proof glass rooms. It will be like box seats, or a limbo room for sinners like the Christie family, and other tormented Catholics with small children.

Markers Make Kids Evil

PART I - THE DESTRUCTION

Remember when studies came out during the 1990s linking video games to the evil behavior of teenagers? I think that theory is wrong. The problem is markers, **permanent green markers**, to be exact. *Permanently* on my new cabinets, stainless steel appliances, new kitchen table ... !%&$! What the heck were the makers of Sharpie thinking when they made a marker that is "permanent on most surfaces" and "quick drying?"

My crime: I go into the bathroom to do something VAIN-*wash my face and brush my hair!* My sentence: Permanent marker all over my kitchen! The scarlet green scribble announcing to everyone who enters: "The Toddler Was Alone Five Minutes."

I make a solution of bleach, vinegar, water, Lysol, Vodka, and every other cleaner I own, while chanting a spell of curses. Then I scrub the doors, walls, table, benches, and finally, little rosy flesh fingers attached to a laughing baby mouth.

All the while I'm chanting to myself: *"It's just permanent marker, no big deal, no big deal, no big ... AHHHHHHHHHHHHHHHH!*

PART II- My Descent into DELIRIUM

Oh yes, a solitary storm cloud descends on the Christie house as I witness the destruction of my beautiful kitchen. Rain is pelting the window as I cry and scrub. Baby Bigfoot approaches me. I'm on my hands and knees dipping a brush into a bucket. He grabs my face with his marker-stained grubby fingers and moves so close up I can feel his breath. His runny nose is touching my forehead and I'm frozen with the scrub-brush pressing the wall.

"Saaa YEEE Mama. No boo hoo." He says, smashing his snotty little face all over mine in baby kisses.

He hobbles off, with a load in his pants, laughing and mumbling to himself as I sit, frozen on the tile floor. I wonder if this boy knows that already he can make me screaming furious in one minute, and then melt me in the next with an apology.

Mommy the Ghostus Slayer

It gets dangerous to bring small children to craft stores in autumn. I'm talking about Halloween season, when retail establishments seem to go overboard on the gore. We're at Michael's again today getting the pieces for another foam Halloween project when I make the mistake of turning down the electronic props aisle. There are ghouls taller than Big Brother on display and my kids freeze mid-step when they see them. I try to be reassuring.

"Don't worry, they're just plastic."

I've forgotten that this idea is foreign to them. After all, big brother holds entire baseball games in his mind, and he is a one-man team. Princess has a magic flying friend who helps her dress in the morning. In other words, to the average preschooler, this store might as well be the Basement of Hell.

Mommy has so much to learn. I'm expecting them to think rationally about Halloween, and be on their best behavior in November because Santa's elves will be watching from our windows. Fear and horror are actually the *natural* reactions that one should have in response to an overboard Halloween display. Like so many other adults, living in the world has desensitized me to violence and gore. It's been about 28 years since I "flew" around the yard repelling evil-doers with my Wonder Woman powers. When did I forget what it was like to think like a child? Luckily, in situations just like this one, raising children helps save me from the disenchantment of adulthood.

Case in point, we're looking at the miniature Halloween village when, suddenly, the monsters come alive. The ghoul speaks.

"Excuse me. Would you like to come in and join the spooky party?" (terrifying laugh)

Princess screams. Big Brother clutches her in a protective hug, looking horrified. Baby Bigfoot is unmoved, staring from his captive position in the front of the shopping cart. The older two start shrieking.

"DO SOMETHING MOMMY! THEY'RE COMING ALIVE!"

Now the grim reaper is gesturing that we follow him, his eyes ablaze. Princess is crying. I walk over to the display, a little upset by the commotion these silly robots are causing. I'm searching for the plugs when I look up at the kids. They're still hugging each other for dear life. Always remembering safety first, Big Brother warns,

"Be careful mommy, the ghostus might get you."

My daughter grows angry, her lips twisting into a little snarl. "BOP THOSE BAD GHOSTUS, MAMA!"

She's throwing punches in the air with the one arm she's temporarily freed from her death grip on her brother.

"Look, they're not real. Watch," I say, as I slap the ghoul across the face.

To my surprise, and secret amusement, he responds:

"I'm sorry. Once you come here, you can never leave!" (ghoulish chuckle)

The kids scream again. Nice move, Mommy. Big Brother's eyes are welling up with tears. He starts to whimper.

"Oh no! We can never leave Michael's and see Daddy."

I finally find a plug, pull it out and show the kids.

"See, it's …," but I never get to the word "fake" because that's when the grim reaper, who's standing beside the ghoul, starts to move his skeletal hand again. His eyes turn red and he's moaning. The kids crash back into their hug, crying, and Baby Bigfoot joins in the melee. He's such a follower!

As one can imagine, now I'm officially frazzled, crawling onto the display platform, searching for a second plug while cursing the craft store under my breath. I'm still foolishly behaving like an adult, determined to show them that these props are not real, when I suddenly flash back to my life as a six year old. I was carving pumpkins with my family. Dad pretended his pumpkin was screaming. It was just a joke, and a funny one at that, but my brother and I became hysterical. That's when I realize that I have inherited my Dad's sense of humor, and more importantly, you can't reason with preschoolers. To restore order in this seasonal aisle, I have to play along. Princess' voice snaps me out of my daze.

"BOP THAT BAD GHOSTUS, MAMA!"

She's swinging punches again. I look down the aisle. No one is there. So I punch the grim reaper in the gut. I'm thinking that I look silly, but, guess what? It's actually fun to beat the crap out of Death. Isn't it interesting how the fears that children battle openly retreat with adulthood into one's dreams? Death has guest-starred in plenty of my own recent nightmares. At that moment I discover that there's something very liberating about embracing one's inner child. In fact, I guess I go a little overboard with the "bopping," because the grim reaper topples over. Big Brother and Princess cheer. Now I see the second plug, and I disconnect it. The reaper goes limp.

"Mama, You did it! You destroyed the bad-est ghostus," Big Brother exclaims.

Princess does her victory dance right there in the aisle. "Yay, Yay, Yay, Yay, Yay, Yay!"

It turns out that, as an adult, I actually get a chance to be a real super hero. I just silenced plastic evil-doers, now I think I'll go home and fly around the yard with the kids. Parenthood is FUN!

Play Date at Hotel California

I enter the kitchen to find my daughter affectionately kissing a carton of orange juice while the dog stands on her hind legs licking the milk and Cheerios out of a bowl of cereal left on the table. Today we have a play date for all three children at the home of my son's classmate. Apparently, my son has forgotten about this arrangement, as he's turned his room into a museum of sorts. He shoves a green plastic magnifying glass in my face.

"Mommy, your job is to find objects that you used many years ago that you can give to my museum. I will examine the objects to see if they are really old."

The pencil tucked neatly behind his ear is supposed to distract me from the fact that he's standing there wearing only his Spider Man underpants. I remind him of our plans and he quickly abandons his research to get dressed.

Meanwhile, I get the other children ready to go. It seems that Baby Bigfoot and Princess always have presents in their diapers at the moment we are supposed to leave the house, and actually getting ready for an appointment takes about an hour of preparation. People who know me have come to realize that I will never be on time. Today is slightly different; I don't really know the parents of the four-year-old we're going to visit. I make small talk with the mother of this friend when I pick up my son from school, and last week she invited us over for a play date. After packing the diaper bag to the point that it is busting at its seams, and agreeing to let Princess wear her Snow White dress over her clothes, we all get in the car.

We arrive at a house surrounded by a white picket fence, set at the top of a steep hill of green grass. I park in the street. The little boy answers the door dressed like a ninja. He's got an extra plastic sword ready to hand off to my older son. The little boy frowns when he sees his friend's sister; apparently, he doesn't like little girls, especially princesses who walk around in Snow White costumes. Before I can even put my bag down the little boy is shouting:

"Chase Princess!"

Princess shrieks in horror and starts running around the house. The boy takes off after her, while Big Brother, truly upset, is running toward his friend, new sword in hand, shouting: "Don't chop my sister!"

Next I'm running after all of them, baby in arms, wondering, where is the adult who lives here?

I find her in the kitchen yelling into the telephone. I say hello and she hastily waves at me and turns her back to resume the phone conversation. It's strange, but there's no time to think. A battle is taking place at the far end of the hall, in the little boy's room. I stop in the doorway to catch my breath. My son and his friend are in the middle of a sword fight, Princess is standing behind her brother, gripping the back of his shirt for dear life. She grabs a Lego and throws it at the boy's head. My first reaction is to scold her, but I have to admit I like the fact that my children defend each other. Now everybody is crying, including Baby Bigfoot, and the little boy's mom walks in.

"Mommy, that princess hit me with a toy!"

The boy is dramatically rolling on the floor while his mother flashes me a dirty look. The end of this day can't come soon enough. Awkward greetings are followed by distracted small-talk in the kitchen while the children play in the adjoining den, which the mom insists is childproof. Her boy is beginning to accept Princess, his newfound respect for girls coming from the realization that this one is not to be messed with. I attempt to give the mom a compliment.

"You have such great hair," I say to her as she puts cold cuts on the table, "it's so shiny. What do you use?"

She looks surprised and laughs. "You think it's real?"

She's lifts her hair off the top of her head. She's wearing a wig. I'm speechless and the mom is laughing in this odd, and very loud way.

"Come on, let me show you my collection," she says, leading me into her bedroom closet, where there are a number of wigs stacked in boxes.

"This is the one I wear to pick up Junior at school," she says while she jiggles the wig in her hand. "I wore it today so you wouldn't be confused."

I am confused, and still at a loss for words. Now I feel terrible because she must be sick and losing her hair. I apologize and she seems to have read my mind.

"Oh no, I'm not sick. I decided I would shave my head and invest in some real quality wigs. It's so much easier."

All I can say is "Oh, wow that's ..."

My awkward response is cut short by the sound of a crash in the den. Baby Bigfoot is surrounded by potato chips and broken glass on the floor. I run to pick him up and look in his mouth. He's alright, but the other kids are not there. Now I'm frantically searching the house screaming my kids' names while this strange lady is following, now wig-less, trying to make light of the fact that three children are missing. My heart leaps into my throat when I see a sliding door at the back of the living room open. It looks like there is a deck and beyond that, an in-ground swimming pool.

I run toward that door, sweating. I feel a sense of relief when I spot the children on the deck huddled around a wooden box that looks like a planter. At least no one reached the pool. The wig lady and I run outside. If not for the fact that my baby is in my arms, I'm sure I would have passed out at this point because I realize that the planter is an ashtray that's built in to the deck. Junior, my son and Princess have used cigarette butts in their mouths. The mom shouts:

"What are you doing Junior?"

I hate to say it, but Junior looks cool. He takes the cigarette out of his mouth and shrugs. "Ma, I'm just having a smoke with my new friends," he says, exasperated.

Now it's my turn for shooting dirty looks, as I grab my kids with my one free arm and pull them into the house to find a sink. The mom is trailing behind me, laughing.

"Junior tries to be just like his father," she explains.

My kids don't want to leave. In fact, survey says, they are just starting to have a lot of fun. They shout in protest, but it's starting to rain and I'm all played out.

"I have to go," I announce, not caring at this point about etiquette.

Princess is kicking and screaming, and she's forgotten how to stand up. Her socks and shoes are missing. I don't bother looking for them. I make my way down the grass hill with her and the coats in one arm, Baby Bigfoot in the other. Big Brother reluctantly follows. Now we're driving home.

"That was fun!" shouts Princess.

"Mama, what's a smoke?" asks Big Brother.

I don't know about them, but I definitely need a nap.

Socks Conspiracy

If I happen to have the misfortune of being hit by a bus, and find myself suddenly matching socks, then I will know I've landed in hell. At my baby shower someone gave me little blue plastic rings. I thought they were napkin holders. Then I found out they are used for matching socks.

"Why will I need help doing that?" I wondered aloud at my Baby Shower.

Now I know why so many seasoned moms laughed at my naive comment that day.

Socks are evil. They have brains and make plans to drive me insane. I have this revelation as I stare at a pile of them. Next I'm matching and folding, remembering the early days of married life when it was easy to figure out which socks were mine, and which belonged to Milk Man. Then I had Big Brother, and it was still simple to discern his booties from grown-up socks. After Princess came along the socks started really multiplying. Still, it was not too difficult to handle the growing pile because her socks were mostly pink.

Then something unusual and creepy happened while I was in the hospital giving birth to Baby Bigfoot. I came home to face an army of angry, mismatched socks, and they soon took over my home. True, I was drugged up on pain killers, but even so, the socks were crazy!

All day long I'm like a broken record speaking to the kids.

"Where are your socks? Put back on your socks. I just put on your socks, now where are they?!"

In church Big Brother starts pointing at the statue of Jesus on the cross and says:

"Look, Mommy, He took off his socks. Where are Jesus' shoes and socks?"

I have no answer for him. Instead, I experience an epiphany. As the choir sings "Be Not Afraid," Jesus sends me a message:

"Woman, you're right. SOCKS ARE EVIL!"

Joy to the Work!

"Love takes up where knowledge leaves off." -St. Thomas Aquinas

Before my life as a stay-at-home mom I taught high school English. Every day for several years my eyes would pass over a sign posted in the classroom: "Smile! Attitude is Everything." My feelings about that sign would vary from inspiration to cynicism, depending on how the school day was going. I became so accustomed to seeing this sign on the wall that I eventually didn't even notice it, or so I thought. Somewhere, on a wall in my brain that sign is still posted, with somebody's chewed gum stuck under the word "Smile!"

Saints have suggested that we do our work with an attitude of joy. That means, not only do we have to smile, but we have to actually be filled with gladness...to teach...to dig ditches...to answer phones ... (insert your job here).

"But the fruit of the Spirit is love, *joy*, peace, patience, kindness, goodness, faithfulness, gentleness, self-control." [Galatians 5:23, 24].

Excuse me, what? Even today? I'm at home folding boxer shorts while listening to the sound of three pairs of bare feet barreling around my dining room table. Meanwhile, I'm trying to cook dinner, help with homework, give baths, clean off the table, iron shirts, etc. I have to smile and do these mundane, never-ending chores with joy?

I'm wondering how I can pull off being joyful when I don't feel joyful. Then my daughter enters the laundry room.

"Hi Mama."

"Hi Princess." I say, opening the dryer.

"Oh, I can help you with that Mama. Wow! There sure are a lot of clothes in here Mama," she says, pulling my soggy pile from the washer. "Oh, I like your underoos, Mama. They are fantastically stun-ting."

I laugh, hard. I follow her upstairs with a basket of folded laundry to find more joy. In her bedroom Baby Bigfoot is seated at her princess tea table, eating a plastic cookie.

"Sit down with us Mama. It's celebration time. It's sunny today! Have some cake." Princess fakes a bite. "Mmm! De-fectable!" she exclaims.

So I sit down and have a plastic dessert. The snack is right in keeping with my diet, actually.

Then I go back to my work: changing bed sheets. Princess follows, helping pull the comforter off my bed. She whistles while she works, "just like Snow White, Mama." We sing the Disney songs together; they are embedded in my brain.

"Mama, you know all the words," says Princess.

It's true, I remember the words, but forgot how to apply them. This little child reminds me.

Smile! Attitude is Everything.

Why should we be joyful in our work? What change does it make? I can only answer that question from where I'm standing. Today Princess got her first report card from pre-school. This is what her teacher wrote:

"(Princess) is a leader through example! I often would sit a more active, less focused child next to her at group time and she, just by listening and doing what is right would sometimes help the child to sit and focus in as well."

It looks like my daughter has the same effect on people at school as she does on me. I try to notice and participate in my children's joyfulness. I'm the first to admit that sometimes, this effort to be joyful is half-baked on my part. Can you imagine what my children would learn from me if I applied myself harder at being joyful in my work? Maybe the attitude of joyfulness in work has nothing to do with changing me, but everything to do with loving others. There's no telling how far that love might reach.

Suburban Wasteland

Big Brother comes running into the laundry room, sliding to a stop in his socks.

"Mommy! The chair is missing! What happened to the black chair that the dog liked to sleep in?"

I tell him I threw that smelly, ripped chair out. Big Brother gasps.

"Mama, we have to buy a recycling bin and stop filling up the world's landfills."

Today at school Big Brother learned about saving the Earth.

Thanks a lot, Mrs. Lock. I'm about to throw away a soda can when, in a heartfelt display of tree-hugging heroism, Big Brother slaps his hand on the garbage pail cover and holds it closed.

"Mama! You cannot dispose of a soda can in the regular garbage. The orange can provided by our friendly Town Animation Department is what each family should use for cans."

"It's Sanitation Department," I correct him with a grin.

Then, the moment of truth comes. Big Brother looks grim.

"Mama, do you recycle regularly?"

I crack under the pressure of little boy scrutiny.

"No, Mommy does not. Mommy is lazy and wasteful, I guess, when it comes to saving the Earth," I mumble.

His eyes widen.

"WHY?!"

I don't have an answer ready so I just shrug. Big Brother puts his hand on my arm, because he cannot reach my shoulder, in a gesture of comfort. "Don't worry, Mama. I will tell you what Mrs. Lock teaches us about saving the Earth and then you will know how to recycle." He bounces out of the room, humming.

I'm standing there with the can in my hand and feeling bad, but not guilty enough. So I proceed with tossing it into the main garbage. It's not that I'm against saving the Earth. I like the Earth and most people on it. I am just really busy.

Later, I'm flipping through a magazine. Celebrities are telling me what they do to *go green*. Jennifer Aniston takes a three-minute shower and brushes her teeth, simultaneously. The next page is a bottled water ad, and she happens to be the spokeswoman. I consider what I can do to *go green*, or at least "get sage." Maybe I'll put the baby in cloth diapers. Not!

I decide that it will take years of therapy to undo my cynicism before I can save the Earth. This is not good because Big Brother is watching me now, and his feelings about the environment are so cute and honest. I hope he stays this way.

Before I go to sleep I make "x's" on the floor with blue painter's tape at the top of the staircase. These are the squeaky spots that wake the baby as I walk out of his room. I notice Big Brother's bedroom light on, and I turn it off, since I think he's asleep.

"Mama! What are you doing! My light has to be on all night!"

I explain that shutting his bedroom light out at night is the first step I'm taking in becoming someone who tries to save the Earth. "I'm conserving energy." I explain. There is a silent pause, followed by a cry of frustration. Big Brother gets out of bed and flips the light back on.

"Mama, you can start tomorrow just by putting cans into the orange garbage."

Do You Speak Princess?

I don't believe in reincarnation, but if I did, I'd put my money on the idea that the soul of Gloria Swanson has inhabited the body of my daughter. Like a silent-film queen of the Roaring Twenties, Princess has been trying to call the shots around here since the moment she decided to attempt a debut before I reached the hospital. She slid out of the womb with a strength and confidence that made everyone present do a double-take. Staring down at her little tightly-wrapped body during one of her first feedings, I predicted she would be a fireball who would blaze her own path in life.

Three years later, Princess has a personality that is much too large for her dainty body. She's a fame seeker who collects jewels. Lately, she has been working on a new language. In the doctor's office one afternoon, I ask her to stay seated.

"Yes, My Highness," she bows and sits, enjoying the surprised laughter of onlookers. Holding up her pointer finger, she flashes her big red-jeweled plastic ring at the waiting room audience.

Like so many child stars, the problems of Princess are many, from her perspective, and there are not enough words in the English language to express her various emotions. Overwhelmed by the lunch choices that exclude her desire for two Dixie cups, she declares:

"I'm cold! I can't find my blankee! The dog ate my cookie! GET TO THE POUND YOU BAD DOG!"

She points the dog to the door, instructing her to begin a journey on foot to the dog pound. Meanwhile, the dog retreats to the corner where she can bark and run in her sleep in peace. Princess is growing more and more frustrated. She tries a scene that probably won her an Oscar in her previous life as a film queen. Her large eyes wide and ominous, she lowers her head, forlorn. Then she spins and drops to the floor, seemingly dead. As I step over her, retreating to the kitchen to eat my pancakes, I hear her shout a made-up curse:

"OH COTCHA-KEETA!"

She gets up and storms up to her room. Princess is dramatic, even while sleeping. When I check on her this time, I notice that a costume change has taken place. She is sprawled out on her bed, dressed like Tinker bell, tightly clutching her magic wand. She must have fallen asleep in the middle of casting a spell on the dog, or me.

Sugar and Spite, We're Starting to Fight

"Sugar and spice and everything nice
That's what little girls are made of
Sunshine and rainbows and ribbons for hair bows
That's what little girls are made of
Tea parties, laces and baby doll faces
That's what little girls are made of" -Author Unknown

When Princess is about to turn 4-years-old, she experiences a sudden growth spurt. Sometime during the night she shed her baby skin and, this morning, she is prancing about, like a miniature lady. I hand her clean dance clothes and she goes into the bathroom and closes the door to change.

"I need my privacy," she announces to Mr. Whiskers, who is shut out of what he believes to be *his* room.

Meanwhile, I look for something containing sugar to stash in my pocket for the wait in the lobby of the dance studio. First I go to the cabinet; I know there are Pop-Tarts there, but I find that they are missing. Next I go to the fridge to grab my chocolate-flavored yogurt. It's gone. I'm not happy. I go to my secret stash - the drawer by the front door- for a Tootsie Roll. THE WHOLE BAG IS GONE.

A lack of sugar does something to my brain. I get irrational and scary. I look over at the portable phone. Maybe Milk Man is trying to teach me a humorous lesson for failing at giving up chocolate for Lent. I'm about to call him when Princess approaches me in a backwards leotard. Two silk scarf headbands are tied around her head.

"I'm borrowing your beautiful lady clips for dance class, Mama." she says.

Norman Whiskers runs by. He's wearing one, too.

"You have to ask me *before* you take something, not after," I explain.

"Oh, SHOCK-A-MOE!" she exclaims, folding her arms and scowling.

After dance class we have lunch and I put her on the den couch to nap. She likes to be wrapped like a baby in her quilt. Then I go make myself some tea. My tea bags are missing.

I call Milk Man. He's in a meeting with the President of the United States. (Not really, but he says it's someone important, so I just imagine that.) I ask my husband about the missing stuff and he denies all responsibility. I can tell when he's lying, even through a phone line, so I give up my interrogation and go back to my chores.

Next I'm cleaning the bedrooms. Princess's blankets are lumpy. I pull them back to straighten them out. I discover treasure: sour yogurt, a bag of Tootsie Rolls, a box of chocolate raspberry tea, a china tea cup, two Pop-Tarts, two silk headbands and my fancy green beaded pocketbook.

"*THIS MEANS WAR!*" I think.

I remove my belongings and replace them with a bag filled with carrots and a box of raisins. Then I go to her cradle and pick up her Biddy Baby who is wrapped so carefully beside a plastic bottle. *I'm going to hide it underneath the covers on my bed, and see how SHE likes it!* That's when I see the reflection of the doll in my hand in her princess vanity mirror and realize how dumb I look. Have I lost my mind? The answer is yes. Don't take away my sugar.

Regaining my senses, I put the baby doll down, gather up my snacks and back out of the room … slowly.

Christie Crumbs

"If you speak the truth, have a foot in the stirrup." -Turkish Proverb

When I awake on the couch, I discover that the older kids are missing and Baby Bigfoot is eating a chocolate chip cookie in his Pack'n Play. The last thing I remember is resting for a minute because of a mid-afternoon headache. The leather sectional has a way of sucking you into dreamland as soon as you recline the end seat. I know I didn't give him a cookie.

Suspicious, I get up and head into the kitchen. I hear Big Brother and Princess dive into the laundry room and shut the door. I put my ear up to the door and listen to them handling the ceramic container that houses the chocolate chip cookies. Big Brother is whispering.

"Here, Princess, put these in your pocket and don't tell mommy. The last two are mine, but you hide them."

I hear her agree to his cookie plot as I swing the door open. They both jump, startled. Big Brother is caught, literally, with his hand in the cookie jar. He's speechless, his little sister frozen at his side, as I confiscate the contraband.

"There's only one cookie left," I say in a stern voice. I filled the jar this morning. I ask Big Brother how many cookies he had, and he stalls, counting on his chocolate-stained little-boy fingers.

"Well … actually, I gave Princess four, Baby Bigfoot one, and I only had … five."

I glare at him. A mom always knows when her child is lying. He corrects himself.

"I mean I had six."

Big Brother shakes his head, grappling with the pressure of keeping the truth from mommy.

"I guess it was all together eight," he confesses.

I stare at his quivering chocolate mustache lips as the two of them struggle through an awful pause, anticipating consequences.

"No snack tonight after dinner for either of you. You have to ask permission before you have cookies."

They both dart past me and disappear again upstairs. Grumbling, I open the kitchen cupboard to put away the jar. There on the shelf are two boxes of Cookie Crisp. I gasp and shut the door. I would never feed cookies with milk to my kids for breakfast. I think it's almost criminal to pass cookies off as cereal. I call my husband on his inside line at work. (*Yes, Reader, it is that important.*) He answers formally, which is my hint that he's in a meeting with the superintendent. I push my agenda anyway because "wife" *always* trumps "boss."

"Yes, Mr. Christie, I have a question concerning the daily nutrition of my children. Are you aware that there are two boxes of Cookie Crisp in our kitchen cabinet?"

His tone changes and I can hear him squirming on the phone. His argument is that they were "buy one, get one free," and how can we deprive our children of experiencing a classic American cereal? I hang up, annoyed and somewhat amused.

After dinner Princess asks for dessert. I remind her that there is none tonight because she and her brother had too many cookies today. She looks across the table at him and he whispers something to her, like she's consulting her lawyer.

"Mama, Big Brother wants me to ask you for a healthy snack instead. We want Christie Crumbs." Big Brother shakes his head, "no," and they whisper back and forth again. Princess clarifies.

"Christie Crumbs!"

I'm confused.

"What's a Christie Crumb?" I ask.

Big Brother chimes in. "Princess just wants some of that healthy new cereal that daddy bought. He takes one of the boxes of Cookie Crisp out of the cabinet and tries to read the label. "Christie Crumbs. See, Mommy, it looks like cookies, but it's cereal, so it's really healthy."

"Wow! Imagine that!" I exclaim.

I take the box from him and get ready to toss it in the garbage. Then I have a better idea. "Let me just take out the part that's not healthy," I say.

I pour the entire contents of the box into the garbage and replace it with a bag of baby carrots. I cross out the word "Cookie" with a marker and write "Carrot" over it. I return the box to the table.

"There, now it's *really* healthy. It's a new cereal by Mommy. I call it Carrot Crisp. Enjoy!"

Mommy the Genius

"Tell all the Truth, but tell it slant"-Emily Dickinson

Jerry Seinfeld is funny, but his wife is a genius, and thanks to her, now I am too. Jessica Seinfeld's cookbook "Deceptively Delicious" is my secret weapon in the War Against Anti-Vegans. It is my own children and husband who are vehemently intolerant of the "Fruits and Vegetable" food group, mainly out of ignorance.

This evening, however, I learn that "ignorance is bliss"... bliss for me, anyway. I stage a major secret attack with the help of my new hardcover general, cookbook.

I put butternut squash in the spaghetti, and no one finds out. They all eat it and the kids rave about the meal.

"My tongue buds love this spaghetti, Mom," Big Brother announces.

I know his stomach is thanking me right now; it hasn't seen a vegetable since he sprayed my cashmere lantern sleeve sweater with rejected Gerber peas at 8 months.

My husband is watching me clear off the table. He knows something is up.

"You have what my Dad used to call a 'shit-eating grin' on your face right now. Why are you so happy?" he asks.

I wait until the kids are far away on the backyard swings.

"That's a pretty sophisticated expression, Christie" I reply. "I'm smiling because I won."

Then I go back to the kitchen without really answering his question. From the sink I can see him inside, still sitting at the table. Now he's looking really closely at the spaghetti on his plate.

"You know, if you poison me, they'll find out through your blog," he warns.

Then I drop the bomb.

"Actually, I'm trying to keep you alive; there is squash in your dinner."

Looking shocked, he puts down his fork. His stomach is thanking me right now. It hasn't seen a squash since, as a toddler in 1973, he spit the pureed vegetable all over his mother's bell-bottoms.

"How could you betray me like that?" he asks, dead serious.

I laugh. "COME ON. It's just squash; I didn't have an affair."

Scraping the food off his plate into the garbage he replies, "Well, *SQUASH* is **much** worse."

Sad Carrots

Reader, you would not believe the hoops I jump through to ensure nutritious meals for my family. Tonight, I spend an hour meticulously adorning steamed carrots with sprinkles to create sad faces, in hopes of "guilting" the kids into eating their vegetables. Yes, this qualifies as emotionally abuse. Maybe. But before you call 911 on me, have that dude with the furry orange hat on *Yo Gaba Gaba* arrested. I'm taking the idea from the sad veggies on his show.

While I'm distracted with this task, the freshwater fish in our tank, who were fed by my toddler this morning, are nibbling plastic hot dogs while tropical storm Baby Bigfoot blows toys, books and light furniture all over the den. When I finish my artistic side dish, I peek inside the room, ready to get mad at the mess, but I can't. Princess is playing "babysitter," rocking her little brother on top of a mountain of books. I can't help smiling at this sweet scene as I put aside the carrots to clean up the toddler tornado damage.

When I return to the kitchen, the veggies are gone and Big Brother is standing beside the empty bowl, caught red-handed feeding them to Hell Hound. The dog wisely runs when she sees me.

"What are you doing? Do I have to call THE MAN?" I ask, sternly.

He shoves his hands behind his back, startled.

"Um, Mommy. Um Mom …The carrots were sad because they wanted to go to the party in my tummy, but I told them that I think they are disgusting, and cannot come…So they cried harder …Then Hell Hound came over to me and invited them to a party in HER tummy, and now they are there and happy again!"

He smiles, weakly, fidgeting with the zipper on his sweatshirt. I walk into the den, where I see Hell Hound is sprawled out on the leather sectional. The party is obviously in progress in her tummy, since she's not sniffing for food.

"It's time for Mommy to attend a party … at the insane asylum," I grumble to Big Brother, trying to organize the mountain of toys and books.

"Do they put faces on vegetables there?" Big Brother asks, innocently.

Feeding Time at the Christie House

Tonight there is a bit of tension at the table. Baby Bigfoot is "feeling his oats" as he approaches 2 years old. He climbs up on the bench and insists on eating at the table with his brother and sister. Being around a cousin who is just an infant has caused him to reflect on his identity.

"Are you a baby, or a big boy?" I ask, spooning dinner onto his plate.

A mixed expression takes over his countenance; it's a combination of cherubic mischief and deep contemplation.

"Baby!" He shouts.

The two older children double over in laughter. They think the fact that the baby is starting to talk is very funny, especially when he gets willful.

"Oh, a baby?" I ask, teasing. "Well, then I guess you should sit in the high chair." I then point to it. (Forgive me, I'm bored.)

Baby Bigfoot shakes his head with vigor.

"NO!" He says in his Cookie Monster voice.

He puts his mashed potato-covered hand on Big Brother's back affectionately, and pats. Big Brother giggles before shouting,"EW!"

"OOOOOH," baby Bigfoot mimics him and laughs.

"Guess what, Mama?" Big Brother says, not waiting for my reply. "I lost my job today at school. The teacher changed everything! I used to be the table manager, but now Sean is and I have no job."

"Oh, I'm sorry to hear that. I'm sure you'll get a job again soon." I say.

Big Brother is pushing the string beans under his napkin.

"I don't know, Mama. There are like 22 kids in this class and we all want jobs. It doesn't look very good for me."

Meanwhile, Princess is flinging her corn at the cat with her fork.

"Well brother, in this economy, a whole lot of jobs are being cut." I reply, imagining adult conversation, then turn to Princess and growl, "Sit down right, miss, and don't throw food!"

"Oh, Shock- a -Dibs!" she shouts.

Then Milk Man walks into the kitchen. The kids leap/fall off their seats to greet him. Big Brother reaches him first and hugs his legs. Princess and Baby Bigfoot want to be picked up. He lifts them both at the same time and cuddles them. Big Brother gives him a high-five.

"What's up, my man? Hey, what's 6+8?" Milk Man likes to play games with Big Brother, and his responses are often really cute.

"That's an easy one, daddy, it's 14 ... and ... and ... and 32+9 is 41!"

Milk Man and I just stare at each other. I start checking the math, counting on my fingers.

The Family That Prays Together...Fights

Princess is an old soul. At the dinner table, she asserts her inner mommy. "Don't be ri-dick-lous! Eat your peas, you silly boy!"

Big Brother laughs in surprise, as he picks up his fork in submission to her commanding tone. Dinner time is a ritual of family life that doesn't always go smoothly at the Christie house. In an effort to develop a routine, I sometimes create more strife.

"Who is going to say Grace?" I ask, secretly proud of myself for remembering family prayer time.

Instantly the hands go up and I grin at that, too. How they know I like raised hands is a mystery, since the fact that Mommy has an actual name and other roles does not compute in their little brains. I pick Big Brother, and little sister falls over in wailing protest. She wants to be the first one. I re-evaluate the situation and decide to let her go first. Big Brother surprisingly does not complain. She begins.

"Hail Mary, Fold of grace, the Ord is wit you.

Blessed are you to the women mumble, mumble, mumble,"

Big Brother chimes in: "That's not how it goes!"

Princess starts to cry, because she's trying to pray. Moaning, she decides to dramatically fall off her chair, landing in an ever-so-delicate pose of distress on the floor.

Moments later, after order is restored and her brother is threatened with a phone call to THE MAN, she finishes in a huff of sniffles.

"Pray for us singers, and I love you at the hour of my deaf. A-men."

Big Brother laughs and I try to look stern. I have no idea what he's about to say in his prayer. He folds his hands like a little cherub:

"I fold my hands, I bow my head, to thank the Lord for the food we have, and are about to receive. I love my family and winning games, but not every time. It's not winning, but how you play the game. Sometimes everyone can be equal, and that's a tie. A tie is good, but winning is more fun. AMEN."

A laugh that I've been holding in escapes, along with some Sprite that I just sipped. The children look serious. "Safety violation!" shouts little sister, pointing.

"Mama, you should never laugh with food or drinks in your mouth, because you can choke," explains Big Brother.

I apologize profusely and then we finally eat.

Chapter 3

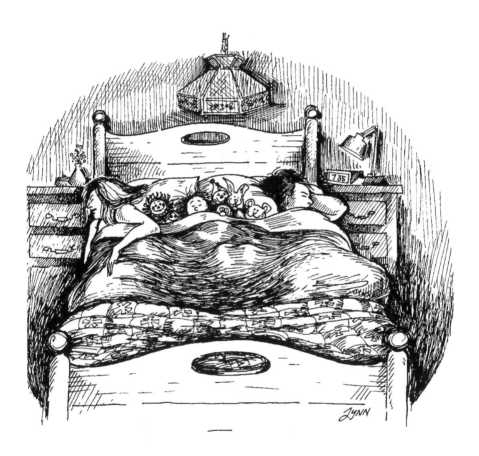

Sleep is on my "To Do" List

"Early to bed and early to rise, makes a man healthy, wealthy and wise." -Benjamin Franklin

This quote pops into my head as I stare at the bedroom ceiling of my youngest child. It's 2:15 a.m. I'm squished next to him in his Winnie the Pooh toddler bed, (temporarily, I tell myself), until he falls back asleep. I want to rise early, but not this early. Heck, I want to be healthy and wise, and yet, here I am, patting this little child in the dark, and the novelty of it all is wearing off. He's clasping my hand with chubby fingers, his eyes slightly open to spy my escape.

I go through the events that led me to this strange sleeping position. First comes his blood-curdling scream, followed by my leap out of my bed that results in a head injury on the dresser. Finally, I'm sliding, perhaps still stuck in the nice dream where I was ice skating on a lake, through the hall to get to his room.

His breath finally steady, and deep, I know I can flee back to my own warm covers, a solid egg shell sheet, no Tigger. I slip ever so carefully onto the floor. Somewhere deep under his comforter a duck is quacking. I crawl backwards out of his room, closing the gate ever so gingerly. He sighs, and I freeze, shivering and praying that I can make it back to my room without waking him.

Clearing his doorway, I run down the hall like an escapee. I know I didn't sleep for two years when I was a child. My parents have told me plenty of times. The truth is I think this is more than just a natural genetic payback. Someone has a voodoo doll.

I Love You, Dairy Barn

"Everyone should have kids. They are the greatest joy in the world. But they are also terrorists. You'll realize this as soon as they are born, and they start using sleep deprivation to break you." -Ray Romano

Rest when the children nap. That's a great idea. I'm about try it on the couch when I feel a kitchen object dropped onto my stomach. I open one eye hoping the child standing over me will think I'm asleep. It's Big Brother with his egg timer. I have to hide that thing. He set it six times yesterday waiting for the babysitter. He knows I'm still awake, and guess what?! He is not tired.

"MAMA! How long will your rest be?" he asks.

I stall for a minute, then reply, "I don't know, five minutes?"

He winds the timer.

"Okay, in five minutes, the timer will ding, I will hear it, and then it will be time for you to get me some graham crackers that are shaped like fish. I'll be back when the timer says your nap is over. Bye!"

He skips out of the room and I reset the dial to 60 minutes. I turn over on the couch and shut my eyes. I'm starting to drift off again when I hear flapping. This time it's Princess and she's wearing her mechanical wings. I can feel her breath as she peers into my face to see if I'm sleeping.

"Mama... Mama! There's a big dragon flying around my room and he bit my hair like this."

She makes a giant motion with her arm, hitting herself on the top of the head. Playing along, I ask, "Did it breathe fire?"

Princess looks grim. "Yes. It burnt my nose," she explains, wide-eyed.

So I scrap the idea of taking a nap and go upstairs to slay a dragon. It turns out to be a little brown moth. I encourage her to try to make friends with it, and head into my bedroom, passing out face first on the mattress. I try that nap idea again, but not for long. I hear the baby cry, and remember that I need to buy milk. I put everyone in the car and head to Dairy Barn.

"Mommy, where are we going now?" Big Brother asks, growing impatient.

"The Barn," I reply, and they instantly understand.

I LOVE Dairy Barn. The person who invented this store is a mom, I bet. In this magical place, I can get groceries without ever taking my kids out of the car. Granted, I've got to spend almost $5 for a gallon of milk, but it's worth it. The teenage cashier is busy eating a cupcake while he hands me change.

"Thanks," I say, adding enthusiastically, "You're awesome!"

He looks confused, because he just doesn't understand what a pleasure it is for me to not have to take my children in the store today. Maybe someone could design a mall that's drive thru? That would really be nice. I look in the rearview mirror and see that everyone is finally asleep. Driving to the dock, I park in a space facing the bay. Ahhh, finally. REST.

My Call of the Wild

"I'm doing a comparative analysis of life as a mother of three young children two years apart in age, to that of a pack of wild dogs."

This has become my canned response to the appropriateness-impaired members of our society who marvel at my "bravery," and feel compelled to ask why I chose to live in a shoe. Remember that book you were supposed to read in high school? "Call of the Wild" by Jack London is about a domestic pet that is stolen and forced to work as an Alaskan sled dog. This previously pampered star must use his primitive instincts and call on his wolf ancestry to survive. I think the same thing might have happened to me when Baby Bigfoot was born. Suddenly, I felt outnumbered by the pack.

Case in point, I'm struggling to eat breakfast this morning. I make the kids toast and myself an egg. I'm trying to eat it really fast, but I get caught by Princess, who ends up eating half my egg. Then I attempt to drink my orange juice, but have to hand it over to Big Brother, who discovers a shortage crisis of this drink in the refrigerator.

Next I go to use the restroom before I have to leave the house. What a mistake. Although I lock the "pups" in the den with a baby gate, they organize an uprising. Baby Bigfoot is hitting the bars of the gate with a toy pot as his sister and older brother chant: "MAMA! MAMA! MAMA! MAMA!"

You get the point. I have to come out of the restroom prematurely. Pack life can be cruel and merciless.

My husband thinks it's odd that even when we go out to dinner I eat fast and with my fingers. Then I excuse myself to spend 20 minutes in the restroom. I'm afraid I'll have to be re-socialized when the kids grow up by the Dog Whisperer. Maybe he has a two-for-one price for me and Hell Hound.

In the street near the bus stop, I pass two old ladies who admire my pack.

"This is the BEST time of your life," one of them says to me.

I try to avoid talking to them, because I haven't brushed my teeth yet. Baby Bigfoot is wiping his nose on my shirt and laughing as I carry him toward the house while steering the now running Princess away from the road. All the while, I'm reciting this mantra: "This IS the best time of my life. This IS the best time of my life."

Sometimes I Remember My Real Name

"It's very, very cold," the children complain as I lead them across the front lawn to the car.

They walk in a line, quacking like ducklings while wrapped in layers of sweaters, hats and puffy coats. Every morning we pretend to be ducks on the way to the car, or the bus stop, because it makes my life more interesting. Sadly, motherhood has reduced my brain activity to that of a farm animal. I strap the "quack-ers" in their seats and off we go.

"Turn on the rock and roll action music!" shouts Princess.

"Hey, what's my name, and how do you ask properly?" I ask this demanding little passenger.

"You are Mommy" the older two shout in unison.

"Mama!" adds Baby Bigfoot, after a three-second delay.

"Right, and my real name?" I ask for kicks, betting they won't know.

They pause, then shout again: "Mom."

I sigh. "No, my girl name. The name I use when I'm just a person."

Silence. Their little brains are stumped.

"But Mommy, that's RI-DICK-OO-LUS. You're not a girl like me, you're just a Mommy, and that IS your real name," Princess offers. "My teacher, Mrs. Caulker, says children have to know their names and phone numbers when they are still kids."

Meanwhile, I'm driving and applying what I believe to be the lip gloss that I just pulled out of my mess of a handbag while still focusing on the road. Stopped at a red light, I glance in the rear-view mirror and realize I'm rubbing a purple crayon from McDonald's against my lower lip.

"You're right," I say, tossing the crayon back in my bag. "I'm just a mommy."

Big Brother chimes in from the back seat, his doughy white cheeks framed snugly by an oversized blue hoodie. "Your person name is actually Loren. That's who you were a long, long time ago, before daddy was born … and you are 29 years old … again."

"Oh." I say, feigning amnesia. "I can't remember that far back."

"That's okay. You aren't a Loren NOW, just Mommy." says Princess.

I look in the rear-view mirror again, and see six big duckling eyes locked on me. At this point I realize that once you're a Mommy, there's no turning back.

House Arrest

Isolation can be a phase of life that makes a person wiser. A stay-at-home mom experiences a sense of isolation, and must come up with creative ways to engage her adult self. Going out and being active, with the children, is very important to maintain sanity. Currently, I own three strollers, and I'm ashamed to say that I have purchased a total of four in my lifetime. None of them are ideal, and that's why I ended up with four. I've got a single, a double, one that a child can stand up and ride on the back, and another double-seater that bit the dust. Big brother spent so much time in the last one that over time, the weight of his growing body actually cracked the frame. I drag one of the survivors outside to wash it down with the hose. It's full of dust from its exile in the basement. As I open the front door, I hear the house alarm beep, alerting the kids, who are playing in the den, that the front door has opened. Big Brother runs to the window.

"Mommy, where are you going?"

"I'm just outside for a minute. Can you keep an eye on your sister and brother?"

Yes, Dr. Phil, if you are reading this, I do realize that I'm asking a kindergartener to watch his younger siblings. Reader, one has to understand that Hell Hound is not a responsible babysitter, so that leaves me no choice. I remember fondly the good old days of reckless, unlimited freedom. I could walk to the shed at the back of my property all by myself, and no one stopped me. Heck, I could even grab a rake and get some yard work done if the whim struck me.

Today, I have to hurry and finish washing this stroller before something goes wrong in the house. Big Brother is jumping up and down at the window.

"Mommy, something terrible and urgent has happened. Come inside immediately!"

I drop the hose and run inside. Baby Bigfoot is eating Princess' oatmeal. He looks up at me and exclaims, "Mmm!" Princess is missing. But, these are not the problems that big brother was referring to. He's playing a preschool game on the internet and the screen has frozen. I put the baby in the play pen for a minute.

"Where is your sister?" I ask.

Big Brother shrugs. To my right is a trail of clothes on the kitchen floor. I follow the trail while collecting shoes, socks, a wet skirt, and wet Care Bears underpants. Then I reach the steps. I call Princess. Her response is: "Sorry Mom. I'm just changing my clothes. Accidents happen!"

As I put her clothes in the laundry, the babysitter rings the bell. Don't arrest me yet, she is a human over the age of 14. Every Tuesday I go to the nursing home to play Bingo, and until my entourage gets older, that requires a real babysitter.

At the nursing home, a dozen elderly folks are watching soap operas in the common room. I smile and greet some as I cross into the dining room where the games take place. Nearest to the television is Bess, a slight woman with piercing green eyes who was a librarian for many years. "That was when I was young," she explains. Her daughter is grown and lives in California. Bess looks down at her hands. After a pause she's suddenly glassy-eyed.

"It's sad," she says.

I take her hand and talk her into joining me at Bingo. We sit with Addie, a Bingo regular. Mike, a war hero, according to his hat, wins five games straight.

"He must be cheating again," I whisper to the ladies at my table.

Bess giggles. At our table, we talk in between games about my children and my fellow gamers' children, grandchildren and great-grandchildren. Addie is the oldest person I've ever met. She's also one of the most joyful people I've ever seen. She fascinates me. During our small talk her eyes light up.

"How blessed you are! The children keep you busy. I remember those days … It's not easy! Before you know it, they'll be grown up and gone. You'll have your own time again."

An alarm sounds in the distance. One of the residents, who suffers from an illness that causes him to wander and get lost, wears a bracelet that triggers an alarm when the exit doors open. A nurse goes over to assist him.

Addie continues. "Do you know how old I am?"

I do. She asks me this question every time I see her. But I say no. It makes her happy.

"One hundred and four years old!" She almost shouts this fact, proudly. She laughs, because, apparently, being that old strikes one's funny bone.

"What's your secret, Addie?" I inquire. I love listening to her, but she has trouble hearing me. I shout my question about four more times.

"Well, I stay involved. I'm on the Resident's Committee. I try to make healthy choices, but mostly, I stay positive. Live in the moment and be satisfied with it, because life changes." "Bingo!" I say, loud so Addie can hear me. Mike looks up.

"This game didn't start yet," he yells.

Addie looks confused. People are grumbling. I apologize to the whole crowd, and then, leaning close to Addie's hearing aide I say: "I mean you're right."

Best Bad Hair Day Ever

I have another one of those "forget to brush your teeth mornings." I know that Brooke Shields never has days like this, as she states in a toothpaste commercial, but I do occasionally. First I oversleep. Then I rush around making breakfast and dressing people other than myself. The UPS man rings the doorbell at 10 a.m. and looks down at the floor when I greet him. Maybe it's because I have a bad case of bed head, or bad breath. I'm sure it's not the robe and pink furry slippers. Actually, I hope it's the hairdo. Perhaps he's just shy.

Anyway, it is a hectic morning. Breakfast becomes brunch, as it doesn't make its way to the kitchen table until almost 11 a.m. I look in the mirror for the first time at 11:15 a.m. The "Mommy ponytail" is my quick solution to unruly hair. Big Brother sits down at the kitchen table. He's wearing his baseball cap. His next comment turns my whole day around.

"You're looking especially beautiful today, Mommy."

I pause in the hallway between the bathroom and kitchen, ponytail holder in mouth. "Why, thank you very much, little man! You just turned my crisscross day into the best day ever!"

He smiles in between shoveling spoonfuls of Cheerios into his mouth. I decide to reward him with a trip to Michael's Craft Store. There, we pick out a giant foam project. It's a haunted house. At home, it takes us three hours to build.

Milk Man sees the completed project proudly displayed on the fireplace mantle when he arrives home from work. He asks what inspired me to have a craft day. I tell him about big brother's adorable and totally sincere comment this morning.

My husband is quiet for a moment, and then spontaneously tells me how beautiful I look, tactfully adding: "Would you mind if I go to a Yankees game on Tuesday?"

New Uses for My Coat

Never, not even in my college days, did I ever sleep in the clothes that I wore all day. I don't even do that while camping. Motherhood, however, is like being on the show "*Survivor*," but with no chance of being voted off the island. This week is what I like to call a "behind the eight ball week." Not only have I grossly crossed the line of neglect in regard to personal hygiene, but I'm also getting pummeled by a slew of parenting and scheduling mistakes.

Yesterday my kitchen was vandalized by markers while I washed my face. I spent so much time cleaning that mess that the dishes piled to the sky, and the den became a Mount Everest of toys and books and … rice? (Oh, wow, I just won't look over there!)

Our house is like Camp Lejuene on a weekday morning. My face pressed to the blue plastic wall of the toddler bed, I arise to the vocal fog horn of Princess who can't find her parents and thinks she's been abandoned. I fall out of the dwarf bed and move my disheveled hair out of my eyes, squinting at the clock. I have exactly 20 minutes to dress myself and three kids, then feed us all before getting my two oldest to school. I'm practically running bare foot on the cold floor, occasionally bouncing off walls, pulling clothing out of drawers, searching for socks that almost match, grabbing bowls, pouring Cheerios, getting juice boxes, tying sneakers and comforting the princess. I slide into the living room in my socks, throwing coats at kids and barking orders. Big brother is assigned "bus watchman" as I change Baby Bigfoot's diaper and bundle him in his coat. Meanwhile, Princess is throwing coasters and watching them smash on the slate hallway near the front door. I should be screaming right now, but I hold it in, remembering it is Ash Wednesday and I have to work on having patience. The bus is coming down the road as I take away the coasters and push the group out the door.

"You deserve a spanking young lady for breaking those and making a mess!" I say as she and the baby climb into the car.

I shut the door and drag Big Brother out to the curb while he pretends to karate chops me. I cried the first day Big Brother went to school on the yellow bus. Every subsequent day since, the bus driver has witnessed my hysterical joy as I wave goodbye to my little tike. Next, I'm strapping Princess into her car seat when I notice her big olive-eyes glassy with tears.

"I'm sorry I broke your china cookies, mama." She mutters.

I sigh, remembering the smashed coasters that were a wedding shower gift. Before having kids I actually used them to protect the table. (I laugh out loud at the thought.) I shrug, deciding that coasters look pretty ridiculous underneath Sippy cups anyway. I kiss her and we hug. That's when I realize: In my dressing frenzy I forgot to put on a bra.

I silently thank God for puffy winter coats that hide free-range breasts as we pull out of the driveway.

I rush Princess into her preschool. I forgot her tuition check. A mom is holding the door for me. I greet her and realize it completely slipped my mind to take Princess to the woman's son's birthday party last weekend. I'd apologize but, I did not get an opportunity to brush my teeth before I left the house. I smile and run away instead.

Back home, I put the baby in his pack 'n play so I can take a shower and change. Oh yeah, and eat. I run through the living room and smash into a suit jacket hanging in a door frame, trip over a belt and slip on a leather dress shoe, landing on the floor. My husband gets home very late from work, and last night he undressed as he walked through the house. This habit of his makes me crazy! I pick up the portable phone and dial his work number to give him hell over it.

"What's up, babe," he says, cheerfully. "Hey, can I call you back? I'm in a meeting." I ignore him because once again, wife always trumps boss.

"No you can't because I'll be in the shower. I almost twisted my ankle just now on your shoes. I should really… spank you like a kid," I growl, truly exasperated.

My husband is silent …Then I hear: "YEAH!"

I hang up. Maybe, if I wrap my coat around my head and spray-paint it white, there is still a chance I can join a group of cloistered nuns in Tibet.

Words of Motherhood

Embarrassed and exposed; that's how I sometimes feel as a mom. Take today, for instance. No, I wasn't mugged. I didn't get caught doing something illegal. I'm just going out with my little ducklings to run errands. Mundane tasks that I used to take for granted, that once seemed so simple, are now a major undertaking. One can compare it to some sort of arctic expedition. That's how slowly we move though each store, holding hands in a line of four, tallest to shortest, like we're braving unchartered territory in a wild, natural landscape. It's just Waldbaum's grocery store.

"What are you buying Mommy?" One asks. "What is it?" Another adds. "What? What? What? MOMMY!" They all shout.

I'm ignoring them because it's private and I don't want to tell them. I do not have the mental capacity right now to explain it.

"Just some stuff for myself," I say.

"What stuff?" asks Princess.

I grab what I need on the shelf and lead them to the register. Unfortunately, Big Brother can read now.

"K-O-T-E-X … KOTEX!" Big Brother sounds out the word on the package and then shouts it. I hush him.

"What's Kotex?" Princess asks innocently, as her Dora the Explorer headband slides forward, covering her eyes. I'm at a loss for words. Big Brother helps me out.

"They look like a kind of diapers," he says.

Princess must verify this hypothesis as she lets go of the people chain to fix her hair. Her brothers and I stop in the produce section, waiting for her. "Is that true, Mama?" She then asks, grabbing hands again. I shake my head in agreement, half-paying attention while herding them onto the checkout line. Big Brother laughs.

"Guess what?!" He yells at the male teenage cashier. "We're buying diapers…FOR MOMMIES!"

The cashier snorts. I can feel the color red traveling up my neck to my face.

"NO Big Brother. The diapers are for our Mommy! THIS ONE," Princess says, pointing to me to clarify this fact for everyone present. The line is long.

I duck down into my coat like a turtle and lead my entourage to the car. Next stop is Petco.

"It's where the Pets go," declares Big Brother.

As one might guess, upon entering store number two, I'm beginning to feel irritated. I'm really trying to keep patient, as the two older kids run off in different directions and the baby throws himself on the floor in reaction to a broken hand chain.

Eventually, we reach the fish. I actually came here to get cat food, but we may never make it to that aisle. We have a freshwater tank, which I recently moved after Baby Bigfoot turned up the heater dial and fried them all. I ask an employee for help, thinking I might get a few fish again. I tell her the story of Baby Bigfoot and the heater, explaining to her that I moved the tank.

"Which fresh water fish are hardier than others?" I ask.

"WELL, a drastic temperature change is going to kill any fish, and if you don't know how to keep a tank, the fish will just die." She explains, in a tone that for some strange reason makes me picture myself smacking her.

I really have no patience at this point for snotty fish experts, as I am already exerting all my energy to keep calm with my children. I'm thinking: "Let's Eliminate Negative Thinking." Then I offer this: "Wrong answer! Have a nice day, Fish Expert."

Then I grab the kids' hands and drag them to the cat food aisle.

"Do you want fish?!" she calls after me, clearly annoyed.

I ignore her, which is becoming a trend today. Then I use my ATM card to pay for the cat food. Big Brother is watching and repeating everything I say to the cashier. He announces the numbers I press on the key pad to the entire line, and I go to cover his mouth out of reflex. He's telling the world my ATM number. Milk Man only found this number out recently, after 10 years of marriage. I might as well be completely naked right now. I really *should* let the kids stay up to watch Seinfeld re-runs!

The cashier is laughing.

"I won't tell," she says.

Everyone waiting to pay reassures me that they will keep the secret, as I run out of the store with my chain gang following me linked together by hands.

Burnt Lollipops: Mommy Made Them with Love

Today I discover that is possible to sleep sitting up, and ruin a perfectly good chocolate lollipop recipe. My chain of mishaps actually started the previous night, when Baby Bigfoot started screaming as if Freddy Krueger was in his bedroom wielding an ax … six separate times. That's right, Zombie Mommy trudges into his room SIX times to comfort him. He wears me out until I break and do the unspeakable Super Nanny no-no. I take him back to my bed on blood-curdling scream number six, at 4 a.m. At this point, I know I am defeated. He smiles and cuddles up with me under the blanket. By 5 a.m., Baby Bigfoot has slid down to my feet, under the covers, and I awake with tears in my eyes, frantic from a nightmare involving him being smothered to death. I pull him up onto the pillow between Milk Man and I. Then I feel his tummy. He's still breathing, and smiling in his sleep. The knot in my throat sinks back down.

The ensuing day is a giant blur. Big Brother's teacher calls and confirms that it is safe for him to bring in chocolate heart lollipops for his class the next day. It's a good thing she does, because I would have forgotten to make them. I decide to do it in the afternoon, before dinner. At 5 p.m. I sit down on my favorite chair with Norman Whiskers on my lap, just for a minute. I'm so tired, and I feel dizzy.

In my dream, Big Brother and Princess are standing over me wearing long curly white wigs, like our forefathers. I'm on trial for something.

"Mama, wake up! You and Norman have slept for hours! The clock says seven, zero, six!" Big Brother starts hitting me with a gavel.

I open my eyes, and discover that it is suddenly dark outside. Mr. Whiskers is still out cold on my lap.

"Seven, zero, six?"

I sleepily wonder what these random numbers mean. Big Brother and Princess lean over me, looking forlorn, minus the George Washington wigs.

"Mama, you forgot to feed us dinner. I'm hungry," Big Brother states.

Princess is whining and rubbing her tummy. That's when the numbers attach to a meaning in my brain. It's past 7 o'clock at night, and I've slept for two hours. I leap up and run to the kitchen. I have a million things to do. I decide to make macaroni and cheese, melt the chocolate for the heart lollipops and get all three children dressed for bed at the same time. The dog is biting my heels; she wants to be fed, too. I run around the kitchen clanking pots, pouring cheese and chocolate.

"There are 23 students in my class, so you have to make 23 lollipops," announces Big Brother.

I only have three molds. I decide to make 15 lollipops, then keep the chocolate warm on the stove while they set in the refrigerator, and make the rest after those are done. I'm sliding Princess' legs into her pajama pants when she screams in my ear.

"Why did you do that?" I shout, ready to scold her.

Now she's shrieking: "Mommy! There's a fire on the stove. Everybody has to GET LOW and GO!"

I turn toward the oven and see my pot of chocolate ablaze. I figure I have two options: grab the fire extinguisher on the wall that I do not know how to operate, or douse the pot with a bag of flour and turn off the gas. I grab the flour and dump the contents of a 5 pound bag on top of my commercial gas oven. Now all three children are laughing.

"Ha, ha! Mama you look like a ghost," observes Big Brother.

"Boo!" adds the baby, in his deep little voice.

It's not funny. Now, my oven needs to be cleaned and I still have to make 10 more lollipops, not to mention put the kids to sleep. *This is not a good day*, I think.

"Who the hell ever heard of burning chocolate?" I complain and swear at myself as I pile the children into the car at 8 p.m. to get more at the store.

The pot ends up in the garbage pail, a casualty of St. Valentine's Day. The kids go to sleep, their books read, by 9 p.m., but it's close to 11 p.m. by the time my stove is clean again. Finally, all the lollipops are wrapped with cheerful tags attached. I crawl into bed thinking that all I really want for Valentine's Day is for the baby to sleep through the night.

As I fall asleep this Black Eyed Peas song is stuck playing in my brain: *"Where's the love, y'all?... Yo! I don' know! ... Where's the peace y'all?... Yo! I don' know!"*

Somebody make it stop!

Throwing Grapes at the Ceiling Fan

I'm driving home from Princess' preschool on a hot, muggy day, and my whiny, tired passengers are melting down when I spot an oasis on Main Street. It's a new spa that looks very inviting. I stop and pull the sweaty, sleeping baby out of the car. My daughter, wearing her Tinker bell costume over her clothes, and her older brother parade behind me, scraping their feet along the pavement in protest. Inside the spa is beautiful and air-conditioned. There are luxurious silk curtains, crystal light fixtures and pink-and-chocolate brown striped walls. It smells like mint. "Wow" says Tinker bell, her eyes wide.

"It's a PINK princess palace!" shouts her older brother in disgust/horror.

The woman at the counter greets me; she appears very well-rested and "together." I accept a brochure from her.

"Hello, I saw your new place and I had to stop in because I NEED A SPA. Just look at me," I offer.

I look down at myself. I'm a sweaty, frizzy mess. The baby is snoring and drooling on my shoulder. The woman pauses to look; so do my two older children and several giggling strangers.

Then the employee laughs, hard.

"I'm so sorry, but we don't serve mommies here," she says. "Honey, you're too old for this spa."

"What?!" The word snaps off my tongue because I'm confused, almost offended.

She explains, "This spa is for girls age 18 and under. We started it for them because they have no place to go to be pampered."

"Really?!" I say.

"Yay!" shouts Tinker bell.

I'm speechless and wondering what young girls do that warrant a day of pampering. "We host birthday parties, especially Sweet Sixteens," she continues.

I leave flipping through the pamphlet and learn that girls can even get limo service to and from the spa. Wow.

In the shop's doorway, a lady stops me and hands me a business card for a "grown-up" spa. She motions towards my entourage with her understanding eyes.

"I overheard your conversation and, as a mom, I know what it's like," she says. "You deserve to treat yourself once in a while."

She winks at the children. I thank her, thinking it is amusing that she's speaking to me "on the down low," like we're old prison buddies. In the car, driving home again, I'm flashing back to my own sweet sixteen party. It wasn't elaborate like some of my friends' celebrations, and I didn't ask for it to be something big. It was in my parents' den. The highlight was a food fight involving the ceiling fan.

Tonight, after the kids are sleeping, I decide to give myself a little pampering. I order pizza and throw pretzels and grapes into the ceiling fan to my heart's content. It is AWESOME until I realize that I'm the only adult around to clean it up. Next year, when I turn 29 again, maybe I'll go to a grown -up spa, one that has ceiling fans.

Chapter 4

The Story of Seven Hours

"If growing up is the process of creating ideas and dreams about what life should be, then maturity is letting go again." - Mary Beth Danielson

That's it? Now I just *leave* and no one is going to *arrest* me? These are my thoughts as I'm standing at the corner near my house, watching my oldest ride away on public transportation. It's the first day of kindergarten and I'm in shock. Unlike Big Brother, who can't wait to start school, I'm not ready for this milestone.

I imagined this day plenty of times. I pictured the pure leisure of it. The empty silence where there used to be whining. The endless requests for drinks, snacks, shoes that need tying, games that need to be reached and played, suddenly silenced- at least for a few hours. I'd get a break from refereeing sibling wars and tripping over sneakers at the foot of the stairs. Just think, I might not have to read *"Stewart Little"* twice today!

I'm standing at the bus stop in a daze, digital camera in one hand, video camera in the other. It seems like only yesterday that I was passing this corner with Big Brother in my shiny new stroller. I wrote a note in permanent red magic marker on the inside cover of his lunch box.

"To a great guy, Mommy is very proud of you!"

He looks suddenly terrified as he boards the bus, glancing back at me as the line of kids prod him along. Now I feel queasy. An older boy takes care of him, sitting with him in the front.

I know I witnessed Big Brother's umbilical cord get cut, shrivel up and, eventually, fall off, but this morning I wonder if it's still attached to me in some way. That would explain why my heart is getting dragged away by the school bus. My nice neighbor, whose four children put homemade cookies in our mailbox when Big Brother was born, is shaking me back to Earth.

"Loren, it's okay," she offers. You can go home now. Don't feel bad. I cried when the first one went to kindergarten."

She's trying to make me feel normal. It's not working, and I'm not crying, but Princess is.

"Where did my own big brother go?" She asks. Oh no, we lost him."

Her upper lip is quivering, a levee about to break. So we don't return home, instead, we walk to the library. After renting the movie,

"*Barbie Fairytopia*" all is right again in her world, and we don't have to be back at the bus stop until almost four o'clock in the afternoon. Not until noon, when I rethink the morning, do my eyes fill with tears.

When the school bus doors swing open, Big Brother bursts out like a bullet. He races home and throws his school bag on the floor in the hall. Next, his sneakers fly off and he wants a snack. Before you know it, I'm mentally calculating how many hours it will be until that wonderful yellow bus will take him away for the day again. I'm heading toward the kitchen to serve a snack when I trip over his sneakers. Landing face-down on the carpet, I'm startled more than hurt. Luckily, I live to pour another glass of milk. When I sit down on the couch, Big Brother slaps a book in my lap. Can you guess which book?

Mama's Still Got It

"I just don't understand it. He stops at THAT house, in the middle of the block, but never at the corner, across from mine, where he's actually supposed to be."

My neighbor, a mother of three like me, is venting this morning about our bus driver. He is an older gentleman, whom I like very much, since I watch him tolerate Big Brother talking his ears off every day.

"He tells me all your secrets," the bus driver joked one afternoon.

I remember laughing nervously, straightening a little.

"I'm surprised you feel that way. I tell my neighbor. "I think he's so nice."

It's starting to drizzle, so I button baby Bigfoot's hat.

"It's the strangest thing." she replies. "He just doesn't like me for some reason."

The bus pulls up as we speak, and the door swings open. The kids file in and the bus driver says to me: "I've been thinking about your walk here. The weather is changing now and it's going to be icy in the future. Where do you live?"

"I'm right next door to the cemetery," I yell over the sound of the motor.

"Okay," he says. "I'm going to stop in front of your house from now on, if you like."

I'm standing there, half shocked, half guilty, glancing at my neighbor who is biting her lip.

"Well, do we have a deal?" he asks.

"Oh, Um… YES!" I step up to his seat at the wheel and hug him. "Mr. Bus Driver, YOU are my hero." I laugh.

"Alright," he says, blushing. "I'll be there morning and afternoon right across from your house … Just have him ready."

I thank him and step off the bus. My neighbor witnesses my touch down victory dance with baby Bigfoot as a pretend football. Meanwhile, the bus has pulled away. I see her expression and grow silent.

She mimics me. "Oh, Mr. Bus Driver, you're my hero!" Then we both burst out laughing.

"YUP, it's all about the CHARM, my friend." I say, looking down at Baby Bigfoot. "Mama's still got it."

Cool Kids Club

Big Brother is stalling instead of going to bed. He's dancing next to me as I wash dishes in the kitchen with the bottle of French's mustard in his hand.

"Mommy, did you know that this mustard provides 40 percent of happiness?"

"No," I say, amused. "Who told you that?"

"The commercial," he says.

I take the bottle out of his hand, flip open the top and pour some in my mouth.

Big Brother watches me, incredulous.

"Yuk! Mommy, what are you doing? Hahaha! That was awesome."

The mustard tastes disgusting without its friends: hot dogs or salami with provolone. My unpleasant observation shows in my expression as I swallow.

"It's time for bed." I say, choking.

"Oh, wow. It didn't work, Mommy. You're supposed to be happy now."

"That's right." I say, returning the condiment to the refrigerator. "The lesson here is that commercials Lie."

"Oh." Big Brother responds, looking thoughtful. Then he comes up with a new topic to gain a few more minutes of bake time.

"Well, I did not tell you about school today. I was elected into the Cool Kids Club. There are 10 boys and two girls in this club."

My eyes widen. Then, remembering he is only six, I feel a bit relieved.

"Cool Kids Club? Do some kids get left out of this club?" I ask.

Big Brother senses my disapproval and immediately throws his friend under the bus.

"Well, that's not up to me, it's up to Michael. He started the club and he's the leader. Today, he made me a Boss of the Cool Kids Club."

"A *Boss*?!" I'm picturing my kindergartner smoking a cigar, holding a machine gun. I check his chin for premature stubble. It's baby soft.

"Yeah!" he continues, quite excited about his promotion. "A Boss can make up the games and be a leader under the top leader, that's Michael."

"Oh," I say, really interested now. "What kind of games?"

"Well, SpongeBob, teeny tiny finger puppet heroes, or rocket ships."

I nod, relieved there is no mention of hits or kissing the ring.

"I really hope some kids who are not in the Cool Kids Club don't feel sad about being left out," I say, hoping he'll get my point.

"Nah. They don't. They just start their own clubs. For an instant, Brandy started the Fast Kids Club and Ryan started the Super Agents Club."

"You mean *for instance*." I say. "Is your friend Riley in the Cool Kids Club?"

"Um, well, Michael asked him to be a Boss, but he said he gots ta think about it."

"Can I be in the Cool Kids Club?" Now I'm playing devil's advocate.

"No. Mommy. I don't think so because you are not a kid; you are an old woman."

"What!? Well, that makes me feel left out. Clubs that leave out people are not very nice." I add the last part because the little dude just called me old.

Big Brother is clearly torn up about the idea of his mother wanting to join the Cool Kids Club. His forehead creases in worry.

"Well, goodnight Mommy." He says, abruptly. A few minutes later I tuck him into his bed and leave his room.

The next afternoon, Big Brother has some news for me as we walk from the bus stop.

"I told Michael that you want to join the Cool Kids Club today, *in secret*."

I try to conceal my grin because he is very serious.

"Oh, did he say I am *in*?"

"Yes and no. Yes, if you bring brownies and 12 apple juice boxes to our meeting, but the bad news is ... since you are a Mommy, you can never make Boss."

"Well, you tell Michael that your mom cannot be bribed. Tell him I 'm so tough that I even eat mustard straight out of the bottle."

"Aw Mom! I'll be the first Boss to get kicked out of the Cool Kids Club. You're so embarrassin'!"

Big Brother the Patriot

Mr. Butler, my elderly neighbor, is an old-school patriot and WWII veteran who is very generous with his summer harvest of tomatoes. I accidently become involved in a political discussion with him this morning on the sidewalk. He's informing me that the government is attempting to rewrite history textbooks.

"Kids are singing songs about the president in school!" Mr. Butler whispers. Looking worried he asks, "What's next?"

I have seen school children singing specific songs about President Obama on television news reports. I admit that this sight made me think:

Hey, that looks kind of weird in a dictatorship sort of way.

Then I just dismissed what I saw, figuring that these children and their teachers were just really excited for and proud of the president. The conversation with my neighbor, however, oils the wheels in my distracted mommy brain.

The next day we are waiting for the school bus to come. I ask big brother a harmless question as he is zipping his coat up to his ears.

"In school do you sing songs about our country?"

"Why, sure we do Mom," he says.

"Like what?" I ask.

"Well, we sing *"My Country Tis' of Me"* and *"Oh Say, Did You See?"*

"That's … great," I say, chuckling nervously. Is it a rewrite of history, or is he confusing the lyrics? I decide he is just being a silly boy. To be extra certain, I question him further.

"Do you ever sing songs about our president?"

"Sure Mom," he says, leaning into my face. Then he puts his hand on his heart and clears his throat. I'm holding in a laugh.

> *"Oh Barack Obama,*
> *We pledge to you!*
> *For your niceness*
> *And your awesomeness*
> *And whatever it is that you do!"*

My laugh slips out in the form of a snort. My son sings like a mini off-key Placido Domingo.

"Is that true?" I ask.

Big Brother looks at the ground and tells me it is. I take out my pen and note pad, which I take everywhere, and write down his song.

"What are you doing, Mommy?" Big Brother is always alarmed when I start recording him.

"I'm writing down your song."

"Okay! I made it up. That last song I just wrote in my head. We just sing the first two songs," he says as the bus approaches.

I tell myself this message that the country is going downhill is just propaganda meant to un-nerve Americans. Every thing he is learning at school is typical and fine.

Later, at his first Tiger Scout meeting, a patriotic discussion takes place following the Pledge of Allegiance. Big Brother raises his hand and is called on to contribute to the conversation.

"Do you know why I love my country of the United States of America?"

(He doesn't wait for an answer.)

"Here we make toilet paper and the best hot dogs ever," he exclaims proudly.

The den mother glances at me, laughing, and I smile weakly. Maybe I *should* find out what he is learning this year at school in regard to American history.

Hunting Cows

The sun is not up yet when I sneak into the shower. My two younger children are still asleep, and Big Brother is busy pacing around the den talking to himself about the possible outcomes of the Colts vs. Ravens football game on Saturday.

Could it be true? Finally after several years of 3 second boot camp showers my children are independent enough to allow me the luxury of taking my time in the morning? My in-the-shower thought is interrupted by an urgent knocking. I yank the towel from the top of the shower door as the silhouette of my oldest appears before the beveled glass.

"Hello? Mommy? Are you in there?"

"No." I say, trying to disguise my voice.

"I know that is you, Mommy. I can see, like, a big mess of wet hair, and your legs and…"

I cut him off. "Okay, what is it?"

"Quick question. I have my January school lunch menu and it says here that today we will be having barbecued ribs, mashed potatoes and green beans. Then I get a choice of white or chocolate milk, or juice or water for kids that are allergic to milk, a fruit cup medley for dessert and a choice of a white bread or wheat bread roll."

"So what's your question?" I ask, patiently dripping.

"My quick question is where do the ribs come from? Is the answer a cow or a pig or a chicken and how do they make ribs out of an animal for my lunch?"

The bathroom door is wide open and I can feel a draft.

"Can you give me a minute to get out of here, and then we'll talk?"

"Um, well, no. You have to make my sandwich right now if I don't want to buy lunch today so I won't be late for school later. So I need to know right now where ribs come from, and then you have to get out of the shower to take care of me."

I'm dancing in my towel, freezing. If President Obama knew what my kids put me through daily he'd have the Christie house shut down for good.

"I think they come from a pig, um, or maybe a cow. I don't know really." I say.

"Oh, so, a cow! Mommy, so men hunt the cows in the winter … but Mommy, how do they get them to be ribs for my lunch?"

I decided when I had kids that I'd always try to be as honest as possible with them. So I quickly summarize the history of the meat industry in the United States.

"The cow is born on the farm; there is no hunting of cows. He is stuffed into a crowded pen with a bunch of other cows he doesn't know. He tells the others to "Mooove" until the farmer can't take his loud mouth anymore. Then the farmer hits the cow over the head with a big bat and cuts him up into ribs, hamburgers, etc. The meat is then delivered to supermarkets, schools, McDonald's, and other places where food is sold. Can you step out of the bathroom now so Mommy can get dressed?"

There is long pause. The bumpy shower glass separating me from Big Brother makes his wide, shocked eyes remind me of a Picasso painting I once saw. The silence is long enough to suggest a parenting mistake, like the time I read *"The Little Match Girl"* to the kids, a Christmas story about a cute little girl who dies homeless and frozen in the rain. I was mad at Hans Christian Andersen for weeks over that ending.

"Little buddy, did you hear me? Does that answer your question, and can I get out of the shower please?"

Big Brother snaps out of his daze. Maybe he was thinking over his feelings for cows.

"Yes, Mommy. Thanks. You can give me lunch money today. I like ribs and cows are born to make them, so it's fine."

As I shut the bathroom door, alone again, I wonder if I should be worried about this little heartless carnivore.

Bed Time Insanity

I run into my daughter's bedroom to break up a fight. Big Brother has Princess in a choke hold over a red plastic telephone with over-sized numbers. A nasal female voice from inside the toy is repeating over and over: "9-1-1, what is your emergency?"

Princess manages to get the receiver near her mouth.

"My emergency is my brother, Mrs. Operator. I need to speak to the President of the United States."

"NO!" shrieks her older brother, horrified.

She speeds up her federal tattle tale as I approach to take away the phone.

"Yes, Hello Mr. Bama. My brother just let the flag touch the ..."

I snatch the toy out of her arms as Big Brother rolls on the floor screaming.

"I didn't mean to do it! I didn't mean to do it!" he yells.

"Do what?" I ask, impatiently. This imaginary crisis is cutting into Mommy's Me Time.

They both start shouting and I hush them. Then both their hands go up. (I wonder, do I have the word "teacher" written across my forehead?)

I call on Princess.

"Big Brother did something shock-ED to the United States flag. He ..."

"No!" Big Brother cuts her off, wailing with remorse. He beats his sister to the punch.

"Mommy, I accidentally dropped the flag on my rug and it touched the floor! The teacher said today at Flag Day that the flag should never touch the floor. Will I be arrested? Will I go to jail and never get snack again?"

I'd laugh, but this child's tears are real. His younger sister, meanwhile, is ready to snitch on him regardless.

"Will he go to jail, Mommy?" She asks, wide-eyed. It seems her sudden patriotism trumps even sibling loyalty.

I fall into a few second day-dream involving Princess. She's clad in a retro youth army hat and pointing at me. I'm frozen with ripped mattress tags in my hands. The *Mommy!* chant breaks me out of the trance.

"What? No. The teacher meant that we should never disrespect the flag of our country. Big Brother just dropped his little plastic flag from school. It would only be bad if he threw it on the floor and stomped on it."

Then comes the "Why?" in unison.

"Because the flag is a symbol, a thing that represents all of the people who gave their blood defending our freedom. It stands for them, and all Americans, past and present."

Blank stares ensue.

"So, I won't go to jail?" whimpers Big Brother.

"No." I say, escorting him back to his own bed.

"Why was that again?" he asks.

Patience Loren, I think. *You are not an asylum warden. They are children and will grow up before you know it ...*

"Well, you won't go to jail for two reasons. One, because you didn't mean any harm to the flag and two, your sister was calling the president on a telephone that is not real; it is not attached to a phone line. She was just pretending."

"Oh. That's right. Well goodnight," Big Brother says, waving his little plastic flag above his bed covers.

Big Brother Is Such a Card

Big Brother is pacing around the den, playing a video game in his mind. He stops at the kitchen entrance I'm busy at the sink washing pots.

"Mommy, why do I have off from school on Monday?" he asks.

I tell him that Monday marks the birthday of a great American, Dr. Martin Luther King Jr.

"Oh, a great doctor who healed many, many people of sore throats and coughs. Wow," he says, earnestly.

"No, not that kind of doctor," I say, struggling to describe the reason we call a person who is not in the medical field "Dr."

"He was a doctor of theology. In 1955, he completed his doctorate degree in college. So we call him Dr. Martin Luther King Jr."

Big Brother is quiet, looking at nothing in particular. I know this means his little mind is thinking about what I told him.

"Oh, a doctor of NOTHING. Just like daddy will be when he finishes school this year!" Big Brother pauses again and then asks: "Will I have to call daddy *Doctor* when he finishes school?"

"No." I say.

He grins. "Will you call daddy *Doctor*?"

I stop scrubbing a pot containing stubbornly crusted spaghetti sauce. "Absolutely not," I say, laughing.

Big Brother runs to the cabinet and pulls out a piece of paper and his crayons. He begins writing at the kitchen table. I ask him what he's doing.

"Just writing a letter. Mommy, What did this doctor do?"

I put down the pot, giving up and letting it soak in the sink. "He wrote, spoke, marched and gave his life for social change so that people of all cultures and colors would be friends."

"Oh," says Big Brother, putting his crayon down. "That WORKED! I have friends of all different names and colors at school."

I smile. Children are so beautifully simple.

"Mommy? Where do I send my letter?" he asks. "Where does this doctor live?"

I frown. Now I have to talk about death. I hate doing that.

"Remember I said that he gave his life for his beliefs? Well, now he lives in heaven with God, his friends, family and the angels."

Big brother looks disappointed. He throws his letter in the garbage pail. "Mommy, can I ask God to thank him for me?"

"Yes, I say, beaming like a teacher who suddenly discovers that her student gets it.

Big Brother cups his little stubby fingers in prayer.

"Dear God,

I love you, and please tell ... Mommy, what's his name again?"

"Dr. Martin Luther King Jr.," I whisper.

Big brother continues.

"Oh, yeah. Please tell Dr. Martian King Jr. that I'm so happy, and my friends of many colors are so glad to have a day off from school! Amen."

Golden Promises

Every once in a while, a mother receives a golden promise. If she is smart, she will save it and redeem it when her child reaches adulthood. These are the innocent, sincere oaths made by children who are, at the moment, quite certain that they will follow through in the future, unaware that these promises are often beyond their adult means.

My younger brother made them to those he adored. I remember one made on a summer afternoon in our grandmother's kitchen. He promised her a new house and a Toyota when he became a man. He was 4 years old. She laughed, delighted. Now in her eighties, grandma still asks him in jest about that promise.

Today I got my first golden promise from my oldest, Big Brother. We were sitting on lawn chairs, melting in the heat of a relentless August afternoon. I could barely move. He was chattering on and on about his future plans as a man. Ever since our trip to the American Museum of Natural History, he's been set on becoming a marine biologist.

"Mommy, what dings will I learn in first grade to help me become a marine biologist?" He asks.

I sigh. His question requires thought.

"Um, well … I'm sure you'll have some science lessons in first grade." I say.

Big Brother is staring at me blankly. That can only mean that a slew of more questions are popping up in his little brain.

"Well, like what, exactly? When will I learn marine biology in spessss…in spesss…"

"Specifically?" I guess the word.

"YES! IN PACIFICALLY," he answers, leaning toward my face expectantly.

"When you are majoring in marine biology in college."

Big Brother sighs and throws his arms up in the air emphatically shouting: "That's way too long from now. Years and years!"

I brace myself for the litany that's coming.

"First, I have to go through being a boy, then a big kid, then a teenager, then a young man in college to finally learn what I wanna learn?!" he asks.

I shrug and nod, because basically, he's right on.

"OHHHH!" he whines. I can see the meltdown beginning as the color red travels up his neck. I wonder if other moms of first-graders go through these conversations about college. I change the subject.

"So, tell me, how old am I?"

Where the hell did that question just come from? I think.

Big Brother looks up at the sky for help. Then he tells me that only I know the real answer to that "riddle" since I always turn 29 every year on my birthday, even though a person can only be a "pacific" number one time.

"So, I guess that you are somewhere in the 30 years and that means that you are an adult woman, going to be a very old woman next, because time is ticking on the clock, and your birthdays keep coming, and your body is getting more tired and soon, BOOM! You'll be in the cemetery, and your soul will be flying up to God."

This speech leaves me expressionless and blinking excessively.

I begin again.

"So, tell me about what you're going to do when you're all grown up."

"Well, Mommy, when I am a man, I will have my own house."

"Oh, can I come over?" I ask.

"Sure!" Big Brothers shouts in my ear. Then he frowns.

"What?" I ask.

"But this is what you can't do, Mommy: Climb up to my bedroom window when I am sleeping in my big man bed, lift me up and sing silly songs to me while rocking me like a baby."

I laugh, hard. He's referring to a children's book called "*Love You Forever*" in which a mother actually does that.

"Oh, no way. I won't do that." I say, knowing that scene scared me too. "But what should I do while I'm over your house?" I continue, as I am getting a kick out of the conversation.

"You just sit down on the couch, watch television and relax, Mommy. I will pour you a cup of wine and cook you some SpongeBob-shaped macaroni and cheese. Then you can take your shoes off your feet and throw them on the floor."

"I can?! Wow!" I exclaim.

"And guess what Mommy?" Big Brother's voice gets low. "I will pick up your shoes for you and even clean the whole entire house."

"Whoa! I can't believe it." I say.

"That's right, Mamma. All you will have to do is NOTHING all day." He says.

Note to self: Remember this conversation.

Alert: Parents Without Dictionaries Shape Young Minds

"If we take matrimony at its lowest, we regard it as a sort of friendship recognized by the police." -Robert Louis Stevenson

Big Brother is playing "college." He holds a heavy book he found, full of dust, forgotten on the basement shelf. After opening it, he points at a random word and asks his father the meaning. Milk Man looks over at the page.

That's "procrastination," he says. Big Brother asks him to explain.

My husband takes him to the sliding glass doors in the den. He points to me in the yard. I'm frantically grabbing things I think will blow away in the coming hours. We're expecting to feel some of the effects of a tropical storm. It's pouring rain outside, and I'm soaked.

"Look at Mommy right now, doing something that should have been done BEFORE it started raining. That's PROCRASTINATION." I run inside, dripping wet. Big Brother tugs on my pants.

"Mommy, daddy says you do procrastination."

"Oh, really," I say, mopping the floor with a towel. Well, you tell daddy that he is the living definition of a closet Democrat."

Big Brother has a confused expression. "What's a closet Democrat?" he asks.

"A closet Democrat is someone who sits around the house, looking to find fault with the person who actually makes decisions and attempts to solve problems around here. He's in the closet because he's avoiding his *Honey Do List*."

Big Brother seriously contemplates for a minute, then accepts my ridiculously flawed explanation, like a good little son. He walks over to his dad, who appears to be reading the newspaper.

"Dad, do you go in the closet and be a Democrat sometimes?" he asks. Milk Man laughs. "Um, that depends … If Mommy is in there, too, then yes."

Mommy Needs to Walk the Walk

"She could never be a saint, but she thought she could be a martyr if they killed her quick." – Flannery O'Connor

This morning is a chaotic rush because the husband was stuck at work until after midnight last night and I have the curse of not being able to really rest when he works late. As a result, I wake up late to Big Brother standing over my bed with a six-page hotel design that he drew in orange crayon. His voice pierces my eardrum because his little mouth is two centimeters from my ear.

"Each person will have a trampoline in his room! Everyone will have ice cream on his pancakes for breakfast in my new HOTEL! Look Mommy, Look Mommy, Look Mommy, Look Mommy!"

I roll towards Big Brother and peer at the clock. In 20 minutes he has to be on the bus, and the dog is missing from my bedroom. I admire his drawings as I leap out of bed, ransack my drawer for clothes and run down the steps to the front door.

I did something very lazy last night and now I'm going to suffer because of it. I didn't feel like taking the garbage out after I changed a diaper and cleaned the cat's litter box. I was tired. I went to bed and left the full bag right by the front door. There were all kinds of toxic waste in that Hefty bag. I just assumed Milk Man would take it out for me when he walked in, but he was just as much a zombie as I was and did not see, or smell it, apparently.

Before I reach the bottom step I see the trail of trash strewn throughout my living room. Last night's dinner scraps, torn tissue paper, and various gross things I'm too modest to mention here chewed and scattered everywhere. I run up to the dog, the notorious HELL HOUND, and drag her out to the yard. Then I come back to the mess, fuming, mumbling curses. There might be fire coming out of my nostrils and it's not the Holy Spirit.

"Don't curse," I say aloud to myself, because I have a parade of children behind me now, gasping at the mess and watching me clean it. I don't want them to say ugly words. I never cursed before I had kids. What the #$% happened to me? I don't know, but I have to change this.

I think it might have been during the delivery of one of my children that I decided that cursing is actually fun. It helps me blow off steam. It makes me feel cool in front of ... preschoolers. What's wrong with this picture?

So I clean up the mess and somehow get everyone where they need to be fully dressed and partially fed. I start to feel a bit calmer because I'm picturing the word "*patience*" in my head. We're in the car on the highway service road paused at a light when Princess screams:"Mommy YOU FORGOT TO BUCKLE ME, AGAIN!"

Yes, she said "again" because I do this once in a while.

"OH SHHHHH ...ocka-dibbles!" I say, catching myself. Princess laughs because I'm speaking her language. Don't meet me at the barber shop yet Britney Spears, I'm trying to do better. I will be more conscious of what I say in front of my children.

We arrive at preschool to discover *that it is closed* today...

Patience, Loren, *patience*. You can do this.

Chapter 5

I've Got My Seasonal Rage Up

It's beginning to feel a lot like Christmas, as some apparently
calendar-less, seasonally confused people in my neighborhood have

begun to put up their holiday lights VERY prematurely, and my Dealing With Rude People Stress-O-Meter has skyrocketed. (That's an invention I just made up that illustrates my seasonally induced public displays of rage.) *Patent pending, of course.*

First I'm in the car driving through my perfectly normal autumn day. (It's early November.)

"We sang God Bless America, my home sweet home, and then Mrs. Hawk took away our flags."

Princess is in the back seat, recounting her day at preschool.

"Oh," I say, genetically unable to resist an opportunity for political cynicism. "Did you tell her she violated your right to freedom of speech which includes the ability to wave an American flag?"

Princess looks confused. "No, silly Mommy, Mrs. Hawk's not a bad witch. She's just my teacher, who gives me water that I like, not juice, YUK, at snack time."

She holds up a photocopy of a cornstalk covered in dripping Elmer's glue and popcorn bits.

"No eat the popcorn, just look at it for art," she warns her baby brother in her most stern Mrs. Hawk voice.

It's not like he can reach her "art," as he is strapped into his car seat. He squirms and yells in a state of infantile frustration.

I stop at a gas station that I frequent because it's self serve only, and pumping my own gas makes me feel liberated and strong … in my minivan. Plus, I'm late for something, as usual. I try to pay at the pump, but the machine keeps spitting my card out. I'm faced with a parenting dilemma. Do I lock the car and go inside the station to get help, or just drive away when my gauge is reading way past empty. I compromise by parking at the pump directly in front of the door, and standing in the threshold of the mini-mart. Then I call the cashier.

"Excuse me, the pump on #3 isn't taking my debit card, and I have children in the car. Can you charge this gas for me?"

I extend my card to him, but he puts his hand up, shaking his head. He cannot even bother to make eye contact with me.

"No, we're cash only."

Now I'm looking back and forth between him and my car outside.

"But I was just here yesterday and the machine worked." I offer.

He repeats himself, louder, as if I'm hard of hearing. CASH ONLY, MA'AM."

That's when I forget I'm watching the car and approach his counter, mad as hell. I'm not sure if it's because he called me

"MA'AM," or if it was the way he spoke to me. Maybe a little of both. Face to face with this sullen person I start in with him because I feel mad.

"If it's cash only, why do you have credit card machines STILL turned on at the pump, and NO sign indicating the change?"

He leans his deadpan expression into my face and responds: "Actually, it's something new here."

Next I'm nose to nose with the guy, growling,

"Well, actually, it's something dumb here."

Then I walk out because I have no Cash on me and my kids are in the car. Driving away I'm wondering why I got so upset at this stranger. Why does this always happen to me in the fall and winter? This is one of the mysteries of being Loren, and I may not ever know the answer.

I could blame this lack of public patience on being a full-time mother of three, but I think it goes deeper than that. When the holidays approach, they bring with them reminders of the importance of being kind and loving. Many times my dealings with people in my life don't leave me feeling warm and fuzzy. That gap between reality and the Hallmark card expectations of the season causes an underlying frustration. I have to work harder to remind myself to try to bring the holiday spirit to others, despite how I feel. Instead of expecting everyone to be walking around wishing me well, I have to become the example of my own expectation. That's hard, and I fail.

Later that afternoon, I fail again. This time I'm walking the kids home from the bus stop, where we picked up Big Brother. I'm carrying the baby, who is struggling to get out of my arms and race with his older brother and sister down the sidewalk. I tell them to freeze, in my sternest voice, because drivers are careless on our block. Big Brother fears me and listens; Princess, on the other hand, fears nothing. She keeps running. There is a gap between us of several feet. I know I won't catch up to her before she reaches the entrance to the cemetery. Meanwhile, someone is turning a car recklessly into it. I scream at Princess, and put my free hand up to wave at the driver to hit the breaks. Princess stops on her tip-toes on the edge of the curb, right before the turning car. I'm running, dragging the two boys with me. Then the driver continues past my daughter and drives into the cemetery. I'm livid, because a child cannot be trusted to stay frozen on the curb. She still could have darted out in front of that car.

I grab Princess by the hand and turn into the cemetery driveway, screaming at the driver, who slows to a stop.

"What are you thinking?! Why couldn't you just wait until I got hold of this kid by the hand? WHAT'S WRONG WITH YOU?" I shout.

Now I'm approaching the back of the car, which has paused in the gravel driveway, and I slam my fist on the trunk.

"WHY ARE YOU IN A HURRY? THESE PEOPLE ARE ALL DEAD! YOU ARE INCONSIDERATE AND CARELESS!"

My kids are standing there, finally frozen without being told to do so. I can see now that a little old lady with large glasses is the EVIL driver, and she looks disturbed by my behavior. She hits the gas and drives further into the cemetery. I'm so angry I could chase her right to some grave, but I turn around and start back toward my house, because I know I just lost my mind for a second.

She's visiting someone who's buried here, maybe a husband, friend or a child. What am I doing, and in front of my kids? I'm not sure, but at times like these, I'm sure glad I'm Catholic. True, I have a bad case of seasonal rage today, but I can cure it after I punish Princess for running near the road, and clear my own conscience for scaring an elderly widow. I'll just stop at Confession after dinner, on my way to Christmas shopping. It feels so good to turn over ANOTHER new leaf. Then I'll be ready to spread some holiday cheer, and tell Santa what's on my own Christmas list: *industrial-size leaf bags and a rake.*

It's Christmas: I'm Getting Good Again

I brace myself for a little holiday shopping, but not on Black Friday. I protest that day every year because it tears apart the whole idea of Christmas, and makes me want to choke on my undigested turkey. This year, I could have "stuffed my bag with blowout sales" at 5:30 p.m. on Thanksgiving evening. Imagine me at the dinner table saying:

"Pass the yams, please, and my coat. Thanks, I have to get to Walmart."

It's disgusting. In addition to the media mockery of Christ's birth, I seem to notice more rudeness everywhere I go, and I have to work extra hard to control my temper. It's like God gives you a test at the holidays to see how mild and forgiving you can be.

I think: *Watch me score a B+ this year in Christmas Anger Management, Jesus! I know I can do it.* (That's a prayer, by the way.)

I go to the mall on a Saturday morning to buy gifts. It goes rather smoothly, until I get on line. To my right is a pile of stuff: bags of bows, wrapping paper and Christmas cards. The box of holiday cards catches my eye. On the front is the image of Mary and baby Jesus. It is one of the most beautiful Christmas cards I've ever seen. I pick the box up just to get a closer look. Then I hear:

"Uh, EXCUSE ME, that's mine."

Startled, I look up to find the owner of the voice. It's this little woman with very tightly curled black hair. Her expression suggests that someone has pinched her. Her arms are full of things and she must have rested the cards on the pile because she was holding too much. I figure this out quickly, but I'm still processing her tone of voice, trying to understand why it sounds rude.

"Oh, they are? The picture is so beautiful." I mutter, handing the box back to her. She literally snatches it out of my hand and struggles to hold it.

"Yeah, well. There is only one box left," she snorts.

I just stare at her. In my mind, cynical me is trying to break out of her chains and speak. I try to mask my thoughts with a smile.

"That's great. Enjoy them," I say. There is no way I'm going to get into an argument with this stranger over her rude tone and an image of the Holy Family. I would not fight over any object in a store, ever, because it's not important.

Wow, I did really well just now! I think, on my drive home. *I passed the first Rude Holiday Encounter with flying colors. I'm going to be much calmer in rude public situations in the New Year. In fact, I bet I will be so mild and peaceful that friends and neighbors will notice.*

When I get home, I open my email. A friend of mine has sent me a question as part of a game.

"If you saw me in the back of a cop car, what would you think I did?"

I tell her I'd guess she was arrested for volunteering too much, because this woman is pretty close to being a saint.

She writes back:

"That is a good one. In your case, you would be in a cop car because someone tried to hurt one of your kids and you went into mother lion mode and beat the stuffing out of that person."

Hmmm. I think it's seriously time to fix my image.

Christie House Christmas Decorating

The kids are busy making foam ornaments for a little mini tree set up in the dining room. We call it our "seasonal tree," because I let them decorate it according to the seasons, and I leave it on a side table year-round. It's a win-win situation for me and them. They spend hours making crafts to hang on it four times a year, and I get a little quiet time.

"What was your favorite part of school today?" I ask Princess as I pass her in the den, in an attempt to distract her from an impending glue fight with big brother.

She pauses, both hands filled with glitter glue sticks, arms raised in the air.

"Well, my favorite part was Jacob," she says.

I pause from cleaning up a pile of Disney books. Big Brother stops gluing to listen.

"Really. Jacob in your class?"

She shakes her head, yes, smiling broadly. It's preschool love, and I've got to hear more. So I press her a bit.

"Um, so, why was Jacob your favorite part?"

She gives up the glue sticks to Big Brother, suddenly wrapped up in the sweet nostalgia of the day's events.

"Today Jacob teased me. Then he chased me all over the grass. Tee heehe!" She laughs, shrugging with glee.

I'm just standing there, frozen in a half-smile by the thought of my baby girl in love with a boy.

"Wow, he must know you are a beautiful Princess." I say.

"Yes, he does … and he's a handsome prince. So, Mommy, we match."

I laugh, then catch her very serious expression and stifle myself.

"Oh," I reply, "Wait until Daddy hears you met a real prince at school."

"That's disgusting." Big Brother explodes, possibly jealous on a sub-conscious level. "Princes are *not* cool!" He's focusing intently on creating a volcano of pink glitter glue on his gingerbread man's face to prevent himself from thinking too much about Princesses.

"Next you're gonna be married." The disdain is clearly evident in his voice.

"Oh, haha he!" laughs Princess, totally liking that idea.

Her joyous reaction to his prediction just makes Big Brother more upset.

"What are you gonna do all day when you're married, Princess? You'll be just like Mama and Daddy. You will just hold hands, and dance the Waltz all day. Then you will stare into each other's eyes and that will make you have, like, 14 babies in your tummy."

I'm at the kitchen sink listening to all of this, and trying to remain expressionless. I interrupt the conversation to hand them tonight's gourmet meal of cheese sticks and noodles. Then we gather haphazardly around the Advent wreath in the dining room. Each of us says a prayer. Big Brother's is a Gregorian chant proclaiming his love for God and the human race. Princess sticks to the old standard, a butchered version of the Hail Mary.

Then an impromptu contest to see who can blow the candle out first ensues, followed by Princess fainting after dramatically spinning in circles to display the magnitude of her horror over losing.

After the kids go to bed I put the large Christmas tree up in the living room by myself, adding up in my head the things I planned to do to make this the best Christmas Decorating Day Ever that never happened: baking cookies with snowman-shaped cookie cutters and three types of toppings, hiding a vegetable in the dinner, and cleaning the toilet today. Oh, well, maybe next year.

The Case Against Turtles

The kids take out a stack of computer paper to write letters to Santa Claus. Since they're occupied and the baby is asleep, I call my husband at work. He tells me to go lay down on the couch. (I have a cold.) I feel so lousy that I take his advice and sit on the leather sectional in the den. That's when the kids put their papers in my lap and order me to be their scribe. So I help them write these long, tedious lists, and they turn out like this:

Dear Santa Claus,
This is what Princess wants for Christmas:
Barbie House
Barbie Jasmine
Princess Aurora
A Cinderella as big as me
A Snow White as big as me
A beautiful, beautiful castle (for Sleeping Beauty)
Barbie and the Diamond Castle DVD
A lovely dress and glass slippers
A beautiful, beautiful, action girl hat
A beautiful, beautiful, beautiful, sparkly queen crown
A beautiful, beautiful, lovely Nutcracker dress

This is what Big Brother wants:
ANOTHER race car and a race car track
A Spider Man DVD
An adventure book
A person with no hair
A humongous fort

AND FINALLY, A secret group gift from Santa, (a real TURTLE)
Wait a minute, I say, pausing the letter. A TURTLE? Reader, I would more willingly find a person with no hair, living in a giant fort and move him to my backyard, than I would go out and purchase a turtle that will outlive me and grow big enough to eat me in my golden years. "Come on, you don't really want that." I tell him.
Oh, but he does.
"Let's just let Santa decide, Mommy." Big Brother says.

Okay, duh, that's me. (I don't really say that.)

The kids take their lists and run off just as Hell Hound flies onto the couch and into my lap. She wants to cuddle, as though she were not man's worst enemy. Surprised by her sudden expression of affection, and weakened by my cold, I give in. I'm petting her, enjoying Judge Christina mock people who make me look like a genius on television. The dog rolls over on her back, and I'm rubbing her tummy when I see it. A FLEA! I gasp, and jump off the couch. I drag Hell Hound by the collar into the bathroom, barricade the door and turn on the bath water.

Next thing she knows she's getting hurled into the bathtub and covered in shampoo. She keeps shaking off and splattering water on me, until I need a bath. So I strip down to my underwear and run out of the room, locking my dirty clothes and Hell Hound in the bathroom until she dries and I purchase Frontline. I look down the hall, the coast is clear, so I run toward the staircase. As I'm running I hear a weed whacker, and then, I almost drop dead in my underwear. The landscapers are here on a day that's not scheduled. Some guy in a Giant's T-shirt is working right in front of the window. I scream. I hear him hit the siding with the weed whacker, obviously surprised. My only saving grace is that we don't speak the same language. As he laughs and mumbles something like an apology, I just run. Upstairs, I want to die. I head into my bedroom and lean against the shut door. Then I hear:

"I love your lovely, beautiful, beautiful, big girl pants, Mama. You look like my naked Barbies."

I nearly jump out of my skin and hit the ceiling. Princess is playing on my bed.

Fully dressed, I hide out in my house until the landscapers leave. I'm still six shades of red, (because I'm a very modest). Then I get the kids into the car and we drive to Petco to buy flea medicine. I find some Frontline for the cat right away, but there is none in sight for dogs. That's when I spot a Petco employee walking down an aisle. So I steer my cart full of children in her direction, but she's moving too fast. Every time I try to flag her down she disappears behind carpeted cat houses, or stacked bags of dog food. I feel like *Alice in Wonderland* when she's chasing the White Rabbit, except I'm more jaded than Alice. When I think I've totally lost her, and can't find anyone around to help me, I have a bit of an outburst.

"Petco sucks," I growl, under my breath.

Then I almost hit the White Rabbit employee with my cart, because she surprises me coming around a corner. I laugh (it strikes me funny that she probably heard me); she does not. Stoned faced, she tells me the Frontline for dogs is behind the registers. I thank her and consider curtsying, just like Alice, but abandon the idea because she's already gone again.

I return home with weapons of mass flea destruction: rug powder and Frontline for everyone with fur. Then I let Hell Hound out of exile. I clean, and change sheets, and vacuum. I find no fleas, but just in case, I turn the whole house up-side-down, figuratively speaking. I don't have wall-to-wall carpeting anywhere, so I don't think they will spread.

Tonight, I'm completely exhausted. Imagine having to feed and care for a turtle on top of all that, I think to myself. NO WAY! I'm thinking maybe Santa can substitute a stuffed turtle. Is it mean to shave Hell Hound completely and put her in a turtle costume? Anyway, that's the case against turtles.

Move Over Santa

After singing two choruses of SpongeBob's ballad, *"The Best Day Ever,"* Big Brother pauses his video game, enthusiastic about beginning his homework project. No, I'm not dreaming, I just looked out the window and decided to keep him home because it's snowing heavily. Princess' preschool is closed, and I can keep him home too because as Mommy, I rule his universe right now.

The bus driver, Don, stops in front of my house and waits for us. Why? Because he's under the spell of my charm, and I pick up that lucky card on the LIFE game board a lot. Either that or he's just a really nice man. I throw my coat over my pajamas and run outside to wave him on. I make a larger-than-normal breakfast for the kids, and they crown me "Greatest Mom Ever" with pink construction paper and glue. As I'm clearing the plates, I make some snow-day conversation.

"So, what do you want to be when you grow up?" I ask, addressing all three children at once.

"NO!" shouts Baby Bigfoot, who is obviously a Toys "R" Us kid.

"A baby doll doctor, so I can tape up all the children who break themselves," announces Princess, after some thought. (We've bandaged her favorite doll, Chelsea, who is made of porcelain, about six times.)

Then Big Brother chimes in. "I want to be Santa Claus!"

His younger sister looks confused. "Silly big brother, there already *is* a Santa Claus."

"Yeah, but he is getting old. I will be his helper, and learn how to drive the sleigh, and I'll take over the job for him."

Princess puts down her hard boiled egg and frowns.

"Can he do that, Mommy?" She asks.

"Those are some big plans. How about you start by just getting dressed and doing your homework," I say.

"Ohhh! Kindergarten is sooooooo borin'!" Big Brother responds. All we do is color, and sit, and write letters, and read, and color again! Let's just skip to college like Steve from Blue's Clues."

"Just eat your eggs, Alex P. Keaton." I say.

Mommy the Home Invader

I love the way the house smells when I bake something that comes out right. My great grandmother's butter cookies are perfect every time I make them. After making a batch, I decide to go run some errands. I put the kids in the car and lock the doors. I go back in for one minute to grab some Christmas cards I forgot to bring over to work. My cell phone rings and I answer it as I'm walking back out. It's a wrong number, so I hang up as I'm closing the door and I just locked myself out. This is what happens when you've got too much going on at the same time in your brain. That's my problem today.

"Alright, let me think this through." I say to myself.

Two of the kids are asleep in the locked car, which is parked in the driveway, and one is at school.

"I'm sure that if I calmly try out all my possible options here, I can resolve this problem," I think to myself, as a cold rain starts to trickle down from the sky.

At least my phone is in my hand. First I jiggle the lock on the front door. Next I kick the door and curse. It's time to regroup. The kids are still asleep, and I call my husband on the cell. He works an hour away. He tells me to break the lock.

"You're strong enough." He says.

Now, I know I have my strengths, and I can open just about any jar closed tightly, but I should never have bought him the first series of *Heroes* on DVD.

"I can't break this doorknob." I say.

He's ready to leave work and drive home. I tell him I'll call him back. I check all the windows on the first floor, and I find one unlocked. The screen has a tiny hole, so I grab a stick and increase the damage until the screen is torn in half. Then I pop it out of the window and lay it on the ground. I try to hoist myself up onto the window ledge and slip, falling into a pile of leaves. That's when I notice a policewoman slowing down in the cemetery driveway next door. She gets out of her car and approaches the fence. I'm brushing dog poop off my slacks, and trying to scrape it off my shoe with a stick. This window is right over Hell Hound's "duty zone."

"Hi, I locked myself out. I'm trying to get in through the window," I say.

The cop looks cautious. She asks to see my driver's license. I get snippy because I'm covered in crap.

"It's in my baby bag, which is in the locked car that also contains my sleeping children. I'm really in a jam here."

The cop is quiet for a moment, and as I listen to the sound of her radio, I imagine myself jailed for neglect. I'm sure I saw that happen to a mom on Dr. Phil's talk show once. I start climbing into the open window again, because it's my house.

"Wait a minute, Ma'm. I'm looking at a ripped screen on the ground here and I need some proof that this is, in fact, your home." The cop's bleached blond hair is pulled tightly into a bun.

I sigh. This is so stupid, and I hate being called "Ma'm." I motion to her, with one leg inside the house and the other hanging over the siding. She approaches me at the window.

"Take a whiff inside this house. What does it smell like?" I ask, exasperated.

"Cookies." she says.

"Right. Butter Cookies. I live here, and I just baked them. I appreciate your concern, but if you let me break into my house I'll give you a whole batch in a collectible tin." I say, forcing a smile.

Her face cracks into a grin. "Alright. Go ahead." She says.

So I fall into my house and Hell Hound rushes into the room, barking and licking my face.

"See, this is Hell Hound. Can't you tell I'm this dog's mother?" I say from the floor.

The cop laughs. I grab a tin of cookies and rip off the attached card addressed to the mail carrier. I hand it to the policewoman through the open window.

"Merry Christmas, Ma'm." she says, walking back to her patrol car.

"She should arrest herself for accepting a bribe," I say to Hell Hound.

Here's the recipe.

Grandma LaCapria's Butter Cookies

- 5 cups flour

- 2 cups sugar

- 5 eggs

- 2 sticks butter

- 1 tbspn baking powder
- sprinkles
- cookie cutters

1. mix sugar, flour and baking powder
2. dump mixture onto a large cookie sheet
3. make a hole in the middle and crack the eggs into it.
4. Add butter, softened, into the hole
5. Squish into dough.
6. Roll out and cut into shapes
7. Bake on greased cookie sheet for 8-10 minutes at 425 degrees.

My List

It's the third week of December and all through the house echoes of coughing and sneezing can be heard. Three young children, plus their father are all sick with colds, leave me wishing for a long winter's nap. Even the dog is sneezing and nursing a scratch she received from the cat (who was not happy to be hit in the ear with dog snot). A general sense of misery fills the air, although the stockings are successfully stuck to the banister with sticky tape and letters to Santa are secured with a dozen magnets on the refrigerator door.

I'm tired and feverish, never really resting because my three children wake up several times each night. I grab a bottle of cough medicine and take a teaspoonful. Then I read the label.

"Controlled substance. Dangerous unless used as directed."

Hmm, sounds...yummy, I think, picturing me sleeping with a smile plastered across my face.

At midnight I'm immersed in a dream involving an eight-month pregnant version of me smacking myself in the forehead repeatedly with a list I once wrote titled: "When I'm a Parent."

In 2003, I put 10 naïve pre-parent promises in writing, because I had read two books on the subject of raising children, and was, therefore, prepared to be a totally awesome, never tiring, always sticking to the rules, never screaming "Here comes THE MAN!" sort of mom. Yes, I was determined to be perfect. Try telling me at the time I might fail and I would have yelled at you:

"Bah Humbug!"

Number 10 on my list was:

I will never let any of my children sleep in my bed.

In the final second of my cough syrup-induced dream, the old list turns into a Thomas the Tank Engine book and suddenly, I'm awake. Baby Bigfoot, now two years old, is standing beside the bed, flogging me with his favorite coloring book. What, toddlers don't create art at midnight?

My legs feel very heavy, but I manage to walk him to his room and tuck him back into his toddler bed, just like Super Nanny advises. In the hall I see the shadow of a girl in the mirror and greet her. Oops, that's just me. Hiccup!

I crawl back into bed too groggy to laugh at myself just as the wind picks up outside my bedroom window. The drip, drip, drip of the rain turns into a fierce storm. Lightening flashes, and then comes the loudest crack of thunder I think I've ever heard, followed by what I imagine is hundreds of angry buffalo charging toward my bed. For some reason, I can't move.

The thunder rumbles again, and I realize that this storm is not a dream. Neither is the stampede. First Hell Hound flies up onto the bed. Next comes Baby Bigfoot out of his bed again and climbing over me, followed by Princess who is in tears. Finally, Big Brother runs into the room as if he is being chased by zombies and leaps on top of his dad who grimaces in pain.

Now my husband and I are clinging to the covers at opposite sides of the bed, nearly falling off. I slide back into a dream. This time I'm hanging down from the plank on a pirate ship full of laughing, naughty children and pets wearing eye-patches.

In reality, the toddler is between us, propped up on pillows with ten of his favorite stuffed friends. The dog is at my feet, snoring and sneezing in her sleep. The two older kids are curled up in the center of the bed with their survival essentials: six Barbies in a convertible and a randomly quacking toy duck. We're like a litter of puppies all snuggled together in a cardboard box. I'm wallowing in self-pity, utterly defeated by Mommy Push Over Syndrome; Super Nanny is scolding me in my mind. I picture my children in their fifties with me and hubby as old people, all still in the same bed. I'm horrified at the thought, but, at the same time, I think that *something about this less-than-ideal sleeping arrangement is actually...nice.*

Super Nanny gasps at my thought. Her disapproving image pops out of my mind like a balloon as my toddler grabs my hand in his sleep and sighs. The rain is still falling outside, but we're all safe and warm.

Oh well, lists are for Santa, I think, pulling myself in from the edge of the bed and drifting back asleep.

Chapter 6

It's Just a Bloody Tooth

> *"Happiness does not depend on outward things, but on the way we see them." –Leo Tolstoy*

In the great adventure of Motherhood, the mundane is peppered with little shocks here and there. This is the case tonight when Big Brother wanders down from his bedroom and approaches me in the kitchen. I am loading the dishwasher. His mouth and teeth are streaked with red, and he's holding something small and white. I'm initially startled, seeing my child bloody, and I think he senses my fear.

"I lost my tooth mommy, see," he says while holding up his disgusting prize. He then notices the blood on his hand and screams.

"Blood! Oh no! Mommy, will I live?" he asks.

I laugh out loud at his sincere concern because I just can't help myself, and someday I'm sure he'll share that with Dr. Phil.

I slip the tooth into a plastic sandwich bag and lean down to his level. "You lost a tooth. It means you're growing up. You *will* live."

The worry on his brow suddenly dissipates as his little mind churns over an important fact he recently heard.

"Will the Tooth Fairy come and give me cash?"

I nod. Big Brother's happy, bloody grin quickly reverts back to a frown as his little brain thinks some more.

"But, but, but, what if the Tooth Fairy is on vacation tonight? Does she take days off?"

I'm wondering why I have to answer these types of questions after 9 p.m. I'm at a loss for words. Luckily, Milk Man is in the room. He reassures Big Brother that the Tooth Fairy has a co-worker who fills in for her if she is out. The substitute is either the Sand Man, or if he's not available, Tinkerbell. That satisfies Big Brother, and all is right again with the world. He falls back into a peaceful slumber in his bed. He's lost one tooth, but I've lost a $10 bill because I have absolutely no change in the house at the moment. When I was a little girl I had to have teeth surgically removed to make that much money. Next time, I'll make sure the Tooth Fairy sends the ghost of Jacob Marley, so I can give the kid a dollar.

The Little Boy Who Laid an Egg

I'm trying to cook dinner, but I turn off the gas oven when I hear a specific type of little boy scream that is different from the regular whiny noises of play.

"Ahhh! Mommy, Mommy, Mommy! I just got cut! My skin scraped off! The dirt got into my muscles and I'm really, really hurt! Help!"

I drop the food, not caring that the very naughty family dog is peering up onto the counter to spy on what's unattended, and run outside. Big Brother is on the ground surrounded by an emergency response team made up of Princess and Baby Bigfoot. They are both slapping him on the back and top of his head to comfort him.I bend down expecting to see peeled skin and blood, thinking I will have to make a trip to the emergency room based on the complaints."Where is it? I don't see anything!" I shout.

"Ahhh!" How can you not see it?! It's a big, huge scrape!" Big Brother shouts in delirium.

On his right knee is a tiny little red line above a scuff mark, a barely perceptible scratch.

Baby Bigfoot looks confused. He has three of those little scuffs on his knee, and he's not writhing on the ground. He bends down in the dirt to press his little pointer finger on the small cut of his older sibling.

"Ah! Don't touch it! Mommy, Now it's bigger! Help!"

In the bathroom, as his siblings help peel off his clothing and run the tub water, he is still screaming.

"Ah! Are you gonna get a Band Aid? Are you gonna put on medicine? OOOH, OW! Oh! Don't bend it! It might be broken, Ow!" Big Brother yells as he leaps into the bath tub with great agility.

He stretches his legs out in the tub and wails, mouth open wide enough for Baby Bigfoot to reach in his mouth and count his teeth.

"Ah! Now I'm like a penguin. I'll waddle to school and never be able to bend my legs, because it hurts! I'll lay eggs on the playground and have baby penguins."

I laugh, because I'm feeling insane from all the screaming, and picturing this scene is as amusing right now as a beer commercial on Super Bowl Sunday. Big Brother finally stops howling. His brother and sister stop patting him. All eyes are on me.

"Mommy! Why are you laughing?" Big Brother looks outraged.

I explain that I've never seen a boy lay an egg, but maybe he is doing it right now since he is fussing so much over a tiny little scrape on his knee. This suggestion prompts an investigation by his siblings, who attempt to reach under him in the bath. They're looking for eggs. Next we're all laughing. Invisible penguin eggs removed, Big brother's agonizing "pain" is forgotten.

Loren Elizabeth Christie   107

Thanks Mr. Stomach Virus

Princess is having a bad hair day.

"My body feels angry," she declares, rubbing her stomach.

She's too tired to put on her "lady clips" and can't find her magic wand. Maybe she's sick. My fears are confirmed 10 hours later, at 2 a.m., when she's vomiting all over her Winnie the Pooh sheets. Big Brother is next, running into the bathroom, exclaiming "Oh no!"

The baby follows suit, and I hold him over the sink as I pat Big Brother, who's crouched over the toilet. It seems that I suddenly have an unexpected and uninvited house guest. Stomach Virus has knocked on our door, and he plans to reach out to every person in our household to complete his mission of spreading germs.

I arm myself with mops, Lysol and antibacterial soap. I even try reasoning with him. "I like germs and I already have too many, but thank you for your interest." I mutter in a state of exhausted delirium.

The sun is coming up now and I'm still wiping the bathroom floor. Stomach Virus watches me from his microscopic hiding place, laughing. He is a cold-hearted germ, and now it's my turn to be sick.

In between caring for three vomiting children and losing my own breakfast, lunch, dinner in what seems to be an uphill battle against him, I'm trying to remember how Stomach Virus got into our house. Did we pick him up at the market, at Big Brother's school, the last play date? Stomach Virus snickers, "You'll never know!"

He's right.

Next, I'm at the end of my rope spooning grape Pedialyte to the baby and taking gulps straight out of the bottle myself. (That stuff tastes awful, by the way.) It's day two of his visit, and Stomach Virus is getting bored. He's successfully knocked the wind out of Princess and Big Brother; they're both asleep on the couch. My husband is doomed, it's just a matter of time before he's next. Even the dog has thrown up.

There is a bright side to all of this, though. On the third day I stand on the bathroom scale. I lost five pounds. Suddenly I'm smiling. I feel better. I take a shower and the kids are starting to get hungry again. That's when I realize I'm winning. Stomach Virus made a mistake, and now he's growing weaker. He didn't think his visit would make me smile. He starts to slink out of the bathroom, down the hall and out the front door. I slam it happily and set the lock in place. I call after him, "Thanks, Stomach Virus! Jenny Craig has nothing on you!"

Potty Hopping

"Once you become a mother you're the frame, not the picture." -
Unknown

I've always avoided public restrooms, because usually they're visibly dirty. I'll turn green before I use one, always waiting to get home. I drove through three states while pregnant and didn't use one. I guess the fear stems from an unhealthy over-awareness of germs. Having children has only made this phobia worse. When Princess was almost fully potty-trained, she's set out on a quest to visit all the public restrooms on the East Coast.

(*Flashback to 2007*)

In a fast food restaurant, Princess tells several diners standing on line about her Tinkerbell underpants. They act fascinated. After we eat, she immediately has to use the restroom. I bring her and her two brothers into the women's room, having to first convince Big Brother that it's okay to go in a door marked "Ladies" even though he isn't one.

Once inside, from the corner of my eye, I see myself doing a nervous, crazy dance in the mirror, shouting: "Don't touch the seat! Don't put your mouth on that dirty wall! GET UP OFF THE FLOOR NOW! Oh, oh, I think I see THE MAN!"

Big Brother giggles. "But Mama, this is the ladies room."

I ignore my oldest, holding him against the wall with my Mommy glare, while clutching Baby Bigfoot in one arm and pulling up Princess' underpants with the other. When we finally exit the restroom, Princess is beaming and I'm exhausted.

"That was FUN!" she shouts.

We go through the same routine at **Barnes & Noble**, only this time she breaks the bookstore golden rule. She brings a book in the bathroom.

"You read this to me, Mommy?" Princess says as she shoves a paperback in my face while I'm sitting her on a seat that I've meticulously covered with toilet paper. It's titled: "*Chimpanzee Politics: Power and Sex Among Apes.*" I put it down on the counter.

"Let's save this one for when you're interning with Jane Goodall," I joke.

Big Brother and the baby laugh hard at my quip that they did not get. Baby Bigfoot drops my cell phone in the toilet just as Princess flushes. Without thinking, I stick my hand in the water to retrieve it. Then my brain realizes where my hand is and I scream. I think, *This is why I had kids - to be challenged!*

A-Cute Case of Torture

It's time for the follow-up visit with the pediatrician for Big Brother. He, his sister and little brother gather up hats, coats, and suitcases of must-have toys and, eventually, file into the car. When we get there, there is a wait in the lobby, followed by a longer wait in an examination room the size of coat closet.

Big Brother is crinkling the paper beneath him, as Baby Bigfoot unravels the roll at the edge of the examination table. Meanwhile, Princess is rummaging through the red box marked: "Bio Hazard." I pull her away and wash her hands, watching Big Brother pull various instruments off clips on the wall. Next he's doing jumping jacks on the scale with Baby Bigfoot, (yes, they both fit on it), and I'm starting to shriek at them. After about 10 minutes locked in this teal green box, with three terrorists, I mean cute children, I'm done.

Where is this doctor? I wonder, annoyed.

Finally, she enters the room and examines Big Brother, pretending not to see Baby Bigfoot thrust his hand into the garbage pail, while his older sister is crawling around on the dirty floor beneath the examination table. Big Brother, suddenly thinking that he might have a throat culture, begins to flail and holler. Meanwhile, the doctor is talking to me, giving instructions about prescriptions and so forth, until I feel like my head is about to burst.

"Excuse me," I say, stopping her to restore order in the zoo cage.

When I have done so, I take a deep breath, smile and apologize.

"It seems that while waiting for you in this little room, I began to suffer from an a-cute case of torture. Please don't lock me in here with children for over 10 minutes ever again."

"They're adorable!" she exclaims, smiling, then rewarding my kids with lollipops and stickers. That confirms my suspicions. The doctor is conspiring with them to drive me insane.

Broken Beanie Babies (and other reasons for today's mental breakdown)

"Patience is a virtue." - unknown

I'm at a Wendy's drive-thru ordering a cheeseburger, French fries and a Coke. I pull around the corner to pay and the window slides open. A woman in a maroon hat leans out to take my money. I can't help but notice how extremely round and large her head is. *It's kind of like a balloon,* I think as her visage smears into a magic marker caricature and the mouth screams: "MOMMY! SNOT! HEEELLLPPP!"

I fall out of bed tangled in a knot of sheets as the dog, who is hibernating in a stolen throw-blanket from my living room, lifts her head in droopy-eyed confusion. Yes, I was sleeping. Now I am suddenly not. My husband, who is not moved by Big Brother's verbal alarm, is probably eating my imaginary cheeseburger right now.

"Do I look like a freakin' owl?" I ask God aloud, the only one awake with me to listen, as I get up to tend to Big Brother who I'm starting to believe is Napoleon, reincarnated.

This morning I'm tired, to say the least. The milk went sour because I put it away in a cupboard. The box of Cheerios ends up in the refrigerator. Big Brother stays home with an ear infection.

"Here Mommy, you take this downstairs so I can call you for food."

My oldest hands me a walkie-talkie set to channel 10. Channel 22 will connect him with the local police. (I found that out last week when Baby Bigfoot responded verbally to a collision on the Long Island Expressway). Channel 10 connects him to me, his Mommy slave. He grins, sans front teeth, as I carry his breakfast into his room on a tray. The grandparents bought this toy to extract revenge on me.

I will most definitely do the same to Big Brother some day. Dr. Phil calls it a vicious cycle of passive-aggressive behavior.

At lunchtime, I get roped into a game of Rummy with Big Brother and Princess.

"Why don't you two play Diego Memory Game instead?" I ask, trying to escape.

"Naw, that's borin'! Only babies who are two years old play that, Mommy." Big Brother says.

Princess shakes her head in agreement with her wise older sibling. After all, she is a woman now, one whole year beyond two. She points out her pink star-shaped clip-on earrings as evidence of her maturity.

"Alright. I'll play cards," I say, gritting my teeth because I have stuff to do.

The laundry is piled to the ceiling. Baby Bigfoot passes by chomping on a whole apple, bundled in a backwards winter coat. His head is adorned with a potty-seat hat. The dog is gathering a group of beanie baby hostages by the side door, and somewhere off in the distance the phone is ringing.

We play two games. My victories are quick and painless, so I think. I really can't help winning. I'd have to be a complete vegetable to lose against these guys. I slam down my second flush and look up. Four eyes are leaking profusely, and accusations of cheating fly.

"Mommy never cheats!" I say, truly offended.

In the hall, on my way to the tissue box, I slip and fall on what feels like pebbles. I scream, horrified. Six beanie babies were murdered by Hell Hound while I sat playing cards. It takes me two hours to vacuum up all of the guts that are splattered all over the first floor of the house. Later that evening I'm still finding little beans on the floor.

By the time the kids are in bed for the night I've completely lost my mind. My husband is upstairs watching television on his new flat screen. As I climb into bed I hear: **"Tonight's Hallmark Hall of Fame Movie: *"Loving Leah"* will return after these messages."**

I look over at Milk Man, pinching myself hard to make sure I'm not asleep again.

"You're watching a Hallmark movie? Okay, I'm awake. Are you leaving me for … some other … man? Just tell me right now because the last 24 hours have been rough and I'm exhausted."

But it is actually true. He is watching *"Loving Leah"* and he's still the same old Milk Man. Finally, it's time to relax, and I could not have prayed for a more perfect way to unwind.

I'm suddenly reminded of the time Milk Man decorated his bachelor pad with lace doilies from an antique shop to impress me.

"My guardian angel might be a gay man … Hooray!" I think, smiling at my husband who is magically entranced by the drippy drama.

In Sickness and In Health: I Swear I Missed That Part

What's worse than a sick kindergartner? This morning I find out the answer to that question: a sick husband. Today, I have Big Brother with his walkie-talkie set up on the couch in the den sneezing snot bombs across the room, and Milk Man upstairs in bed ringing me on the intercom. He feels achy and horrible, so he stays home from work. Then he puts in his breakfast order.

Now the dream I had of the bizarre encounter at the Wendy's drive-thru is making sense. It was a premonition. It turns out that I'm the woman whose head pops off her body like an exploded balloon as she takes my order. I answer the intercom.

"Hi, honey. I'd like a scrambled egg sandwich with cheese, a coffee and a cold glass of water with ice."

I make his breakfast and bring it up on the tray that I wrestled away from Big Brother.

"Why are you taking away my tray? I'm still sick. I NEED A TISSUE FAST," Little Napoleon yells.

I dodge the snot grenade and hand him a tissue. Then I clean the tray and carry Milk Man's breakfast upstairs. I can tell he's feeling much better, and he most definitely had a virus last night. It turns out that Milk Man is "milking" his situation. He smiles and presses his covers flat in anticipation of the breakfast tray. I can suddenly see the resemblance in his face to his son. I hand him the coffee and tray, and turn to leave the room, making the mistake of looking back at him as I exit. (You'd think I'd know not to do this after reading so much Greek mythology.)

"Um, did you put milk in this?" He's frowning into his favorite coffee mug. I take the mug and stomp down the stairs, grumbling.

By noon he's downstairs, answering 81 emails from work. I must have cured him with my vegetable "witchcraft." That's right, Readers, I put yellow squash in his scrambled eggs.

The Angel in the House is Sick, Go Away

"You may not know what I mean by the Angel in the House. I will describe her as shortly as I can. She was intensely sympathetic. She was immensely charming. She was utterly unselfish. She excelled in the difficult arts of family life. She sacrificed herself daily. If there was chicken, she took the leg; if there was a draught she sat in it. ... Killing the Angel in the House was part of the occupation of a woman writer. " -Virginia Woolf

It finally happens. I've been sneezed on, mid-sentence, and I've tasted it. Snotty tear-streaked faces have left mask-imprints on my shirts. My house is infested with misplaced used tissues. The kitchen counter has become a makeshift medicine cabinet. First Big Brother, next Princess, then the husband, and finally, even poor Baby Bigfoot is stricken by the germs.

Today it's my turn, and I'm very sympathetic … for myself. I'm congested and achy. I don't want to get out of bed. This Sunday, is Super Bowl Sunday. I sit in my favorite chair like a grey statue, eyes closed, seeing the blurring repetition of white moldings in the darkness. The wall color changes as my fever hits 103.

No, we're not having a Pox Party -- that would be strange and barbaric. It's February and I have three young children who pick up germs everywhere. We have the usual unwelcome winter guests of the upper respiratory variety. Even if everyone is sick, life goes on. The house is cleaned. The laundry, and maybe the ironing, is done. The snow on the walkway is shoveled. Meals happen. Everybody is happy, until I get sick. Then, everything goes downhill. The house gets dirty enough for the kids to notice. Goldfish crackers become the breakfast, lunch and dinner meal of choice. It's every man, child, and pet for himself in the Christie house.

I crawl into bed and pull the covers up to my ears. I can't move. Milk Man comes home from work early and makes me go to the doctor. The diagnosis is definite: Mucus is kicking me in the rear and I need drugs.

I want to be *The Angel in the House* for my children and husband. Instead, I'm the Oscar the Grouch/Wicked Witch. Despite being educated in the ways that great minds have despised the image of *The Angel in the House*, I long to revive this stereotype anyway. Virginia Woolf is turning over in her grave. I set the bar at impossible heights.

Then, I wallow in self-pity from under two blankets, counting on freezing fingers the ways I perceive I've fallen short today in various relationships and duties. Outside, snow is falling in a windblown slant. Life is canceled when Mommy is sick. I move myself to the den couch, so I can appear present and alert. Princess piles blankets and toys on my sick self. She's taking care of me. I feel defeated, depressed even. I think winter needs to leave ... now. The angel's wings are withered from exhaustion.

The garbage smells. The stench permeates my deviated septum and reminds me that I am alive. Something in the pail may have died. I trudge out through the snow to the trash cans with a blanket wrapped around me under a coat. That's when I see it springing from the ground. A crocus bulb is peeking through the blanket of leftover fall leaves. I reach down to touch it: tangible hope. "Hold on, cheer up!" I think. Spring is coming. You'll have your wings back soon enough.

Note:

The title "The Angel in the House" comes from a lyric poem in four parts by Coventry Patmore. Written in 1854, it describes his saintly wife and their ideal marital relationship. In the 1800's, this poem became very popular, and set unrealistic guidelines for Victorian women. By the twentieth century, women began to resent this ideal image of the role of wife and mother, and believed it to be, in many respects, untrue and unfair. This idea is reflected in the writing of Virginia Woolf, whose psychological struggles are no secret.

Keeping Perspective

"When I hear someone sigh that life is hard,
I am always tempted to ask, 'Compared to what?' " - Sydney J. Harris

It seems that I really didn't know the meaning of the word "anxiety" until I had children. It was 5 a.m. on a freezing morning in February 2003, and I was surrounded by flowers and teddy bears in my warm hospital bed. I plugged a little bottle into Big Brother's mouth, watching his big blue eyes locked on my every move, as he made those funny little newborn sounds that come with contented eating. It was in that very cozy moment that an unwanted thought entered my mind, a thought that both horrified and distracted me from the feeding so that I began to give my little recipient too much, and he spit up a bit. While I was staring at the wall, very peacefully, I noticed a sign over the sink: *"Please wash your hands to avoid the spreading of germs."*

Germs. They surround us, and we cannot see them. It was as if I had invented the idea right then and there, and I became upset at the thought that my child can get sick. I know it sounds silly, but after the feeding was over and I sent Big Brother back to the nursery, I lay there until the breakfast tray came, unable to rest. The thought of something happening to my children is my greatest nightmare.

Five years later, I sit on Big Brother's bed in the wee hours of the morning watching him breathe. His night-time coughing fits make it impossible for me to sleep, I find myself filled with anxiety. This tormenting feeling came to a head last April, when Big Brother was hospitalized with pneumonia. Somehow, the germ had traveled into his blood. I found it difficult to eat while by his side in the hospital; I was so nauseated by seeing him hooked up to an IV, and his little name written in a slot next to the door. The day we were admitted Big Brother's never-ending fever broke in the middle of the night, and I cried from relief. It was a nightmare, but not as bad as what some of the parents in the rooms around me faced. The pediatric floor of a hospital can be a sad place, although the staff tries to create a cheerful atmosphere. In the playroom we decorated Big Brother's IV pole with red feathers and twisted pipe cleaners. He named it Hughie, and the pole became his friend.

The next day, my husband called me and said that Princess was also sick with a double- ear infection. Hanging up the telephone in my son's hospital room, I called the nurse in. Then I burst into tears, crying on her shoulder like a child. I could not even form words for several minutes. It was just an ear infection, but I was overwhelmed with anxiety, and exhausted from staying in the hospital. There was no way to split myself in half and care for Princess at home, and Big Brother. There was also the thought that Baby Bigfoot, who was under a year old at the time, might be next with some unforeseen sickness.

"You're actually on the good side of this floor, remarked one doctor who examined Big Brother. "The children on the other side are chronically ill."

He was trying to comfort me, clinically, and he was right. The boy in the bed next to big brother was mentally disabled, and mute. He suffered coughing fits at night, which led to nurses coming in to pound his chest rapidly. He had no mother sleeping next to him, no visitors at all, and it broke my heart. I learned his name from a sign on the foot of his bed and spoke to him briefly when no one was in the room. All night I had listened to him drowning inside his own chest, and more than once I found my eyes tearing for him in my broken sleep. I put a teddy bear inside his covers, but he was unaware. In the room beside ours, there was a sick newborn. Her mother stayed in the room all night, rocking her.

When Big Brother was released, my husband carried him and his little duffle bag, sprinting down the corridors and out into the parking lot. We closed the car doors thanking God aloud for Big Brother's recovery and for being able to leave the pediatric floor.

Everywhere I go I hear mothers speak of sicknesses far worse than what I have experienced with my children, and I wonder how they cope with the stress. To me, some of the most awe-inspiring people are those who have to endure the death of a child. How do they go on? As a new mother feedinw my son for the first time, I was horrified by the thought of losing him, afraid that the loss would break my heart. I suppose this fear is selfish, in that I'm more afraid of how I would face the tragedy than the event itself.

Being surrounded by sick children in the hospital helped put my situation into perspective, though it did not calm my nerves. I try to always remember that for every trial that I face, there is always someone out there who has come through far worse. I never understood the image of the Blessed Mother with swords in her heart until I had children. Now, that picture is a comfort to me. With faith comes the acceptance of a lack of control over our fate and the fates of the people closest to our hearts.

Why am I so nervous about a cough when the parents of other children face all kinds of horrible suffering? The question causes me some embarrassment, because I like to present myself as the picture of strength, but my feelings are what they are. I give Big Brother an extra blanket and an icy drink, and soon his coughing fit subsides. I climb back into bed, this time counting my blessings and not sheep, until I finally fall asleep.

Chapter 7

I Forgive You, Gandhi

Gandhi interests me. I like a lot of what he says, though some parts of his life I find very strange. I quote him all the time. My favorite Gandhi quotes are: "Be the change you wish to see in the world," and "My life is my message."

When I was pregnant with my third child, I read Gandhi's book "My Experiments With Truth." His exploration of humility fascinated me. "I'm reducing myself to zero," he wrote, in describing his ongoing struggle to reach perfect humility.

Reducing to zero, just imagine that. I decided that Gandhi had given me the key to what it takes to be a perfect mom/wife (or insert role here). I decided that selflessness equals happiness. Well, I never was good at Math.

Let me tell you what this quest did to me: it wrecked me physically and mentally. By the time Baby Bigfoot turned 8 months, I was sick. It felt like PMS all day, every day. I couldn't function normally. I was irritated, absent-minded, and more nervous than I had ever been in my life. I had no negative feelings toward my children, but they would ask me far too often, "Mommy, why are you crying?"

My slobbering answer was, "I just don't know."

Maybe it was because I was alone with them for 14 hours a day, and then up with a baby half the night for months. I've heard that sleep deprivation is a form of torture. My husband was doing good things for our family, working, going to college at night and on the weekends. Being able to afford staying home with my children full-time is a blessing. Yet, some days I was so tired that I dreaded the sunrise.

Things I had always enjoyed eating suddenly made me sick. Milk products, chocolate, all the good things in life put my stomach in turmoil. I lost a lot of weight in a short time. (I was glad about that!) I went to my ob-gyn and he raised his eyebrows when I stood on the scale. I said I didn't feel good, giving him details that led to a sonogram. The results were normal. I was just stressed.

I got sicker. There was a pain in my side that just would not go away. I went back to my doctor. I agreed to disgusting, uncomfortable tests involving gallons of chalky drinks, dye injected into veins and tubes in the … never mind. A biopsy was done on a little piece of my small intestines. Everything came back fine.

My nerves were raw. Even when I had a chance to sleep, I couldn't. I was afraid to eat. Something was very wrong with me and after all that, it still wasn't resolved. I went back to the ob-gyn and finally saw my favorite doctor. (She delivered Princess and has known me since I was 17-years-old.)

Sitting in on the examination table, I told her how mixed up my life felt. I told her how stressed and sick I still was.

"I just want to give my children 100 percent of my energy, and I fail, miserably. I think I forgot how to use the restroom! I'm trying to be selfless, but I hate it! I gave up everything I was before they existed. I wanted to reduce myself to zero to be a great mom."

When I stopped, my doctor was staring at me.

"Who the heck told you to do that?" she asked.

"Um, Gandhi ... I think?" I muttered, smiling weakly.

Then she gave me a hug and said: "Well, Loren, Gandhi is wrong this time. Now, listen to me. I've been delivering babies for twenty years, and you are not a strange case. I'm telling you right now to take back 25 percent for yourself, and give them 75 percent."

My eyes widened.

"That's right, you're going to hire babysitters, take breaks, explore hobbies, interests, talents ... and seek help. Take care of yourself, so you can take care of them. It's time you try something new and get healthy again."

I left her office relieved. I listened. I changed. I did something for myself. I took back 25 percent and guess what? I realized the hard way that tending to yourself makes you better equipped to deal with stress. Caring for yourself enables you to be good at all your roles. Duh?

I forgive you, Gandhi, and thank you for teaching me to love myself as much as I do others. By the way, can you babysit Saturday night?

Revolting Against Myself

I put on my sneakers and head out the door. Milk Man puts down his book.

"Where are you going?"

He's wondering because it's dark and raining. The kids are in bed for the night.

"I'm going for a run. I'll see you in 20 minutes."

"You mean a jog," he corrects me.

"No, I mean a RUN." It's okay, he knows I'm weird and prefers me that way.

A revolution is a fairly quick shift in power. (See, Mrs. Ringle, I didn't forget.) This is what's going through my mind as I run in the rain. This is what I need to do for myself:

1. Identify the patterns of thought and habits that are draining my energy and potential.
2. Declare war on those things.

Hours of daily self-reflection are the fruits of being a stay-at-home mom. It's not that I'm not busy, but it's not like I shut off my brain and stop thinking when I'm cleaning the macaroni and cheese off the wall. My brain feels idle a lot although my hands are very engaged. My cynical, negative imaginary friend likens it to working on a factory assembly line. The angel on my shoulder says it's such a blessing to be fully present to savor the little ones! I feel somewhere in the middle of these opinions, occasionally shifting more towards one or the other, depending on how my day goes.

I like to day-dream that I'm on the verge of a big and exciting shift in my life. On one hand being home full-time forces me to read more, and contemplate the direction of my life as I sit in neutral, raising my kids. However, I've discovered that I don't like having so much time to think, because for me, thinking leads to change in my life. I'm not comfortable with change. I want to run from change.

I was the thoughtful daughter who didn't make mom wait up too late. I am terrified of being selfish, inconsiderate, a failure. Guilt has a way of controlling me. I'm the play-it-safe girl who never ventures past the line of waves in the ocean regardless of how joyful the people swimming beyond them look. I dig my feet in the sand, my chair wedged on the edge of foaming water teasing my toes. There are invisible things about me that I dislike.

I have to change. The patterns of thought, fears and weaknesses I've been able to ignore in previous roles parade across my mind like giant red worker ants distracting me as I read "Cloudy With a Chance of Meatballs" to the kids. They giggle and wrestle, oblivious to Mommy's little mental struggle.

Today is just as good as any other to start living unapologetic and boldly, I think as I run past my house for the third time. I look toward the driveway, pretending I don't drive the minivan parked there. The light in the upper hall window looks so inviting and cozy. I run faster. This is the first act of my personal mini-revolution. No, I'm not leaving my family; are you crazy?! I love my kids more than life and my husband is the greatest man in the world. I need to break away from my old self and change on the inside.

Today I planned out a garden. I marked the dirt with line chalk and flipped it over with a shovel. It felt good to dig out the space. Then I added more topsoil and started planting seeds. My mud-covered children helped press the tiny pellets into the dirt. They had a blast. I lined the edges with berry bushes: blueberries, strawberries and raspberries. In a few weeks the center will have vegetables and the sides will have fruit. When we were finished we soaked the garden with water; the kids lined up behind me holding the hose like firefighters. Meanwhile I was thinking about how I used to pick the raspberries in my grandpa's backyard, and my grandma and I would wash them, and pile them into a cream-colored bowl. I planted sunflowers in the back row because I love beautiful, defiant WEEDS, and four-O'clocks in the front (a flower from my childhood). Next to the sunflower seeds are foxgloves and hollyhocks, a reminder of my dad's garden.

When I was done I felt so good! Running and gardening … how does this change me into someone I like better? Perhaps it's my active attempt to dramatize spiritual and emotional growth in my life. If not, at least there is the possibility of getting back the old Loren body that turned people to stone in her bathing suit.

The Freedom to Move

"Go confidently in the direction of your dreams. Live the life you have imagined." -Henry David Thoreau

Today is Princess' last day of Dance Camp, and she and her new friends put on a little show for all of the parents. There is a solo part that each of the girls had where, one by one, they danced any way they like across the room. The song was *"Kiss the Girl"* from The Little Mermaid soundtrack, in which all of nature swells up and urges the prince in the story to take a risk. My daughter is the last soloist. Oh, how she flutters and waved her arms. It is very cute. She is bold and joyful because she believes that she is a dancer.

Even more than being entertained by her routine, I am really mesmerized by her innocent confidence. It is beautiful.

"Before you can teach them anything, you have to give them the freedom to move," explained the dance instructor. This line floats around in my mind all day. It was a very important sentence, I tell myself. I even write it down in the car on a gas station receipt and put it in my wallet next to a note from my father.

Later, on the beach at Fire Island, I am watching her relive her performance in the sand from a distance, and I'm thinking again about her sureness. I have a sudden wish that I could capture her attitude in a little bottle, the kind with a cork that one finds washed up on the shore in stories. What a treasure it would be to have that mindset for life! Then, when society hits her continuously with false messages like a storm battering the sea shore, dulling down the sharp edges of her confidence, she will not change the shape of her dance. My Princess will still move "confidently in the direction of her dreams." Thoreau's words are my wish for my children, myself, and every one for that matter.

The dance instructor's words are tossing around in my thoughts. "First give them freedom to move…"

There is an odd looking shell fish stuck on its back near the water after being misplaced by a wave. Its greenish-white legs are flailing in the sun, and it cannot right itself. I instinctively pick it up and throw it back out to sea, because I don't like watching it struggle.

Perhaps the water will carry the creature right back up to the hot mound of sand, and it would be stuck there again. Who knows, but only with its legs on the ground can it move. So at least, it is set in the right direction.

As they grow up, I want to be able to discern how I can help my children when they seem stuck, while maintaining their freedom to move. I want to have enough faith to throw them back out into the ocean, so they will find their own unique way of moving across it.

Chasing my toddler across the sand away from people's golden retrievers who, unlike my youngest, have a basic understanding of how to stay near their human families, I begin wondering. Who sets me back on my feet when I am stuck? How do I know when my feet are on the ground again, and I am free to move? How do I keep the innocent outlook of a child so I will be courageous enough to progress in the direction of the "gentle whisper?"

"After the earthquake came a fire, but the LORD was not in the fire. And after the fire came a gentle whisper." (1 Kings 19:12)

A lot can be learned from finding your own way in life, and learning to let others find theirs.

Generation X Homemakers: We're Not Your Mom's Mom

The idea that I initially had about married life and motherhood adjusted itself after I had children. Up until that time I had been holding on secretly to idealistic notions of what I could achieve, but it was futile to try to be the living, *liberated* embodiment of the 1950's stereotype. Still, stubborn as I was, I had to try it.

When I was focusing on my career I made a lot of rigid plans about the kind of mother I'd be in the future. Like so many other women, I struggled with the idea of balancing work and raising children. I liked having a career of my own and when children came along, I was tested to follow through on my lifelong personal promise to put that life aside and dedicate myself to them. This sacrifice was harder than I thought it would be, but in my heart I felt sure that it was the right turn for me to take at that point in my life.

When I left work to stay at home, I got two reactions from others: envy or distaste. Some people would say: "Isn't it great to be at home with your children? Cherish it!"

While others would frown and comment something like this: "What do you do all day? Aren't you bored?"

At first I resented the second comment. It wasn't for some time that I realized that both ideas held some truth in the reality of the homemaker's life. Of course, a person with an active brain, although she cherishes her children more than life, cannot focus solely on raising them. It just is not healthy. One needs creative outlets, and other roles that enrich her life, or else she feels shriveled up and, finally, invisible.

Thank God society has finally acknowledged the fact that women are intellectually equal to men. This is why today's homemaker looks nothing like your mother's mother. I'd like to brag that I have all of the qualities of my grandmother, but I think I'd be lying. There are two things that I lack as a homemaker in the 21st century: patience and submission.

I acknowledge that I need help. I need breaks. I need showers more than once a week, nice shoes and clothing sans drool stains to wear once in a while when I make a guest appearance in my role as my old self: Independent, Well-Dressed Career Woman. I may stay at home, but my husband is expected to help me raise the children and it is not a societal faux pas, as it was for grandma.

Yes, I embrace my role as a mother and wife happily, but I haven't put aside my creative dreams. I am not a silly little housewife who gets into mischief, like the main character from *I Love Lucy*. I am a strong-willed person who needs to keep her brain busy. If I want to "sing in the show," like Lucy, I'll do it, even if I don't get a chance to brush my teeth and arrive on stage with baby snot on my shirt.

My grandma ironed grandpa's T-shirts. This fact is a reminder that I will never be her. The truth is, I *hate* to iron. My husband accepts that and presses his own shirts. He's a lot kinder to me than I am to myself. That's true love in the 21st century, my friends.

Gratitude Is My New Favorite T-Shirt

"Let us be grateful to people who make us happy; they are the charming gardeners who make our souls blossom." - Marcel Proust

I'm one of those people who believe that life's events are not random. There is a plan and I'm part of it. I think the portions of my life that seem bland actually contain invisible purpose. I decide I'm going physically put on Gratitude every day as if it were a piece of clothing, no matter how I feel. I'll "dress" my mind in gratitude so I can keep this perspective front and center in my thoughts. I think this idea might actually change a stubborn, cynical girl like myself for the better. Why shouldn't I be grateful? I should, but it is easy to forget one's blessings when engaged in the humdrum, day-to-day routine.

I start one morning when I open the curtains in my den. I can see real signs of spring in the backyard, and this is a cause for joy. There are bulbs emerging from the soil, and the familiar songs of spring sung by the seasonal winged inhabitants of my yard have started to return. Birds remind us to be joyful.

I smile as I close the curtains and return to my miniature Camp Lejuene. Big Brother is dancing around in his underwear instead of getting dressed for school and Princess just attempted to kick the cat's tail. I scold them both and put Princess on the steps for a time-out. She will not apologize to Norman Whiskers, nor will she even agree that kicking animals is naughty.

As I sit her on the time-out step she shouts a made-up curse: "OH, SHOCK- A -MOE!" Then, feeling remorse, starts crying softly.

Big Brother is dressed with my help, and after his coat is buttoned, I relieve Princess from her confinement in time-out. She has already forgotten the whole episode. I watch their sibling morning ritual. First comes hugs and kisses. Then Princess turns into Gary, SpongeBob's pet snail-cat.

"I love you Gary. See you later!" shouts Big Brother.

"MEOW!" Princess replies.

Sometimes in the middle of the parenting chaos I stop and wonder:

Dude, Where am I?

Despite the challenges of parenting, the answer is always the same: I'm exactly where I'm meant to be and I'm grateful.